THE MERS OF SAURASHTRA REVISITED AND STUDIED IN THE LIGHT OF SOCIO-CULTURAL CHANGE AND CROSS-COUSIN MARRIAGE

About the Author

Dr. HARSHAD R. TRIVEDI was born (1923) in the village of Hariana in the Jamnagar District of Gujarat State (India). His student life was spent in Baroda where his family migrated during his childhood. He received Ph.D. Degree in 1955 from the M.S. University of Baroda, Department of Sociology under Prof. M.N. Srinivas. Subsequently, be worked among the Dubla Halpati and Naika tribes of South Gujarat for about a year in the Tribal Research Unit of Gujarat Research Society of Bombay.

In 1957, he joined a research-cum-action project of environmental sanitation under the joint auspices of Delhi School of Social work, Ministry of Health and Ford Foundation in New Delhi. He later shifted to Mussoorie to join National Institute of Community Development as Deputy Director in Cultural Anthropology until 1964. This marked the end of his regular employment for good. Today he is the author of a dozen study reports-books, both in English and Gujarati most of which are published. Presently Dr. Trivedi is Honorary Secretary and Director of Institute of Cultural and Urban Anthropology, Ahmedabad.

The emineant administrator-scholar, Shri T.N. Chaturvedi, says: "I first met Dr. Harshad Trivedi in Mussoorie in 1962 as a member of the faculty in the National Institute of Community Development which later on shifted to Hyderabad. I hardly knew him then as one who is inclined to work on conceptual and theoretical formulations despite remaining outside the façade of ostensibly impressive formal academic life. Even at present, he seems to be moving in between applied and pure social research, a kind of adaptability and intellectual resilience he has acquired over an unusually long period of chequered career as a social scientist. All these years I have had the opportunity to meet him occasionally and read some of his valuable papers. Dr. Trivedi has contributed a good many learned research papers from time to time to scholarly and professional journals in this country as well as abroad."

THE MERS OF SAURASHTRA REVISITED AND STUDIED IN THE LIGHT OF SOCIO-CULTURAL CHANGE AND CROSS-COUSIN MARRIAGE

HARSHAD R. TRIVEDI

CONCEPT PUBLISHING COMPANY PVT. LTD.
NEW DELHI-110059

The Indian Council of Social Science Research gave the financial support towards the publication of the Work. However, the responsibility for the contents of the book—facts, opinions, conclusions, etc.—is entirely that of the author and not of the ICSSR.

ISBN: 978-81-7022-044-2

First Edition 1986

Published and Printed by

Concept
Since 1974

Concept Publishing Company Pvt. Ltd.
A/15-16, Commercial Block, Mohan Garden,
New Delhi-110059 (India)
T: 91-11-41101460
E: publishing@conceptpub.com, *W*: www.conceptpub.com

Dedicated to

Outstanding Social Reformers of the Mers who spear-headed a ceaseless drive of literacy and education to uplift the community.

Late Shri Maldev Bapu Keshwara

A freedom fighter of distinction

Late Shri Moldevji Odedara

Former Finance Minister of Gujarat

and

Hon. Shri Vijayadasji Mahant

Agriculture Minister of Gujarat

FOREWORD

The Indian Council of Social Science Research, New Delhi has provided teacher/scholar award of fixed grant to Dr. Harshad R. Trivedi to enable him prepare this monograph. We are grateful to the ICSSR for the same.

Harshad R. Trivedi made an indepth study of the Mers of Saurashtra for the award of Ph.D. degree thirty years ago from the M.S. University of Baroda. It is now recognised as a valuable contribution by international standards. The Mers (or Mahers) are mainly peasants settled in the Porbandar region of the Junagadh District in Gujarat.

The initial study (1961) was made indepth as per the tradition of structural-functional theory of social anthropology. It had its own limitation as most theories have in social sciences. In this study, Dr. Trivedi has laid emphasis on exploring social, economic and cultural changes among Mers owing to technological revolution affacting the lives of the people. The author comes to the conclusion that inspite of apparant changes in manners, dress, housing and other physical aspects of life, the importance of the Mer kinship organisation and lineage structure has not at all diminished.

If there is any change in the structural relationships among the Mers, it is of microscopic magnitude within the caste. Their vertical relations with other castes in the village are affected due to introduction of new technology and out migration of artisans for earning livelihood. The kinship organisation of the Mers is not under strain so far on account of technological invasion from outside the system. The author predicts that young educated Mer boys and girls might become choosy in the years to come and avoid preferencial cross-cousins for the purpose of marriage. Dr. Trivedi has adopted advanced theories and concepts to analyse and interpret his data. It has enabled him to throw valuable light on the functioning of the Mer Society and the system of cross-cousin marriage under historical circumstances and contemporary times.

The Saurashtra region of Gujarat has many such living historical societies with rich cultural heritage. They call for urgent scientific studies before they wear out their age-old cultural ethos. Dr. Trivedi deserves to be congratulated for this theoretical work of lasting academic relevance. I hope that the scholars will be pleased to react to it favourably.

Higher Secondary Education Board, R.S. TRIVEDI
Government of Gujarat. *Chairman*

PREFACE

As LUCK would have it, I left Delhi to settle down in Ahmedabad after two decades of sporadic research assignments in the Central Government departments and also outside. I would not have taken up the Revisit study of the Mers had this not happened. I feel that it has become a blessing in disguise. I hope and trust that this monograph shall vouch for it.

The purpose of the study is clear from the title of the monograph. The objectives as laid down in the design of the study form a composite theme woven around bilateral form of preferential cross-cousin marriage and the impact of change on social, economic and cultural life of the people. Most of the data used here came from field observations and secondary sources of information. Each chapter of the monograph tries to deal with a specific theme or part of an objective determined for the study. Additional information has been presented in the two appendices derived from the survey report prepared by me in 1981, for the Backward Class Board of the Government of Gujarat.

I am grateful to the Member Secretary of the ICSSR, Dr. D.D. Narula for the grant-in-aid offered to me to work on the old subject of my abiding interest and specialisation. My thanks are due to Prof. M.S. Patel, and Prof. R.S. Trivedi, the former and present Presidents respectively of I.C.U.A for encouragement. Shri Jivabhai Keshwala, the President of Junagadh District Panchayat Samiti, and the prominent Mer leader, provided necessary help and encouragement in the study for which I am highly obliged. Shri R.D. Gandhi gave valuable assistance in preparing the manuscript, while Shri Jethabhai Visana of Ahmedabad and Shri Gigabhai Atabhai of Porbandar, both the enlightened young Mers spared their valuable time to provide useful information for this work. I am grateful to them all for the help.

HARSHAD R. TRIVEDI

CONTENTS

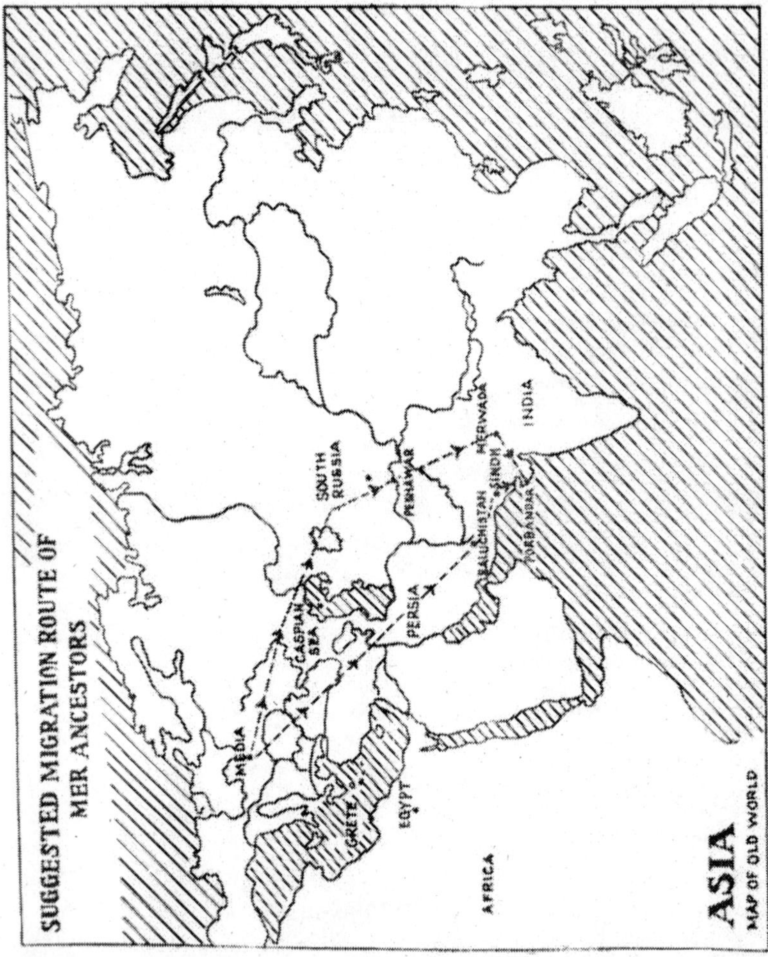
SUGGESTED MIGRATION ROUTE OF
MER ANCESTORS
MEDIA
CRETE
EGYPT
AFRICA
CASPIAN SEA
PERSIA
SOUTH RUSSIA
PESHAWAR
BALUCHISTAN
SINDH
MERWADA
PORBANDAR
INDIA
ASIA
MAP OF OLD WORLD

1

IMPACT OF ECOLOGY AND TECHNOLOGY ON THE LIVES OF THE MERS

Introduction

SINCE a substantial period of more than one generation has passed away when I undertook the first study of the Mers, a background note will be appropriated at the outset of this monograph.

Initially, I visited the Mers as a field-worker for two months to explore possibility of studying folk arts of the Mers in the summer of 1951. I had however to give up the idea of the study of folk arts due to various reasons. The area where the Mers are concentrated was formerly ruled by the princely State of Porbandar, located on the coast of Saurashtrian peninsula of India. This first visit was followed by three more field visits of longer duration at different points of time until the close of 1954. In all, I spent a little less than 12 months for the field work to study the social structure and organisation among the Mers. The study was sponsored jointly by the Departments of Archaeology and Sociology in the Facutly of Arts of the M.S. University of Baroda for the award of Ph.D. degree.

The total number of villages, covered for participation-observation field-work at that time, amounted to 52, i.e. about 35 per cent of total Mer dominated villages in the area.

I had no occasion to get in touch with the Mers for about 30 years until the revisit in 1980 to conduct a socio-economic survey sponsored by the Gujarat Backward Class Board, Gandhinagar. During this long period of sojourn, I was in Delhi for more than 20 years (1956-76) and was engaged in various kinds of applied work for community development covering normative and behavioural socio-cultural dimensions of research. It was a chequered carrier, but to my mind, not fruitless or unevenful.

For it inspired me to try my hand on theoretical and conceptual nature of research in the areas of planned development, urbanization and social change.

The present revisit in 1984 has come in quick succession to the previous one made in the middle of 1980. I am grateful to the Indian Council of Social Science Research, New Delhi, for the award of the grant to write this theoretical monograph. The monograph is based on critical review of my earlier studies, documentary research and field observations.

At present the highland and lowland areas of the Mer region are divided into three talukas under the administration of the District of Junagadh. Besides these administrative changes, there were marked social upheavals also. I found that some of the old Mer informants-cum-friends had passed away. A few of them however were fairly aged but active and eager to provide valuable information on various aspects of my new interest. Those whom I had seen as kids were in their youths and did not feel shy to talk to me on the innovations they had introduced in their life style including family planning practices.

The indepth data and information which I was able to collect during the present short visit and documentary studies have been incorporated in this monograph. Some ideas and perspectives which were contained in an inspiring personal letter from Prof. McKim Marriott of the Chicago University in 1971, have been of great value in the preparation of this work. They helped me to take up special readings of literature connected with the development of latest trends in the study of anthropology, social changes and cross-cousin marriage. Despite my limitations and inadequacies, I have made an attempt in this monograph to throw some new light on the social organisation and structure of the Mers, covering the following aspects.

1. Ecology, Technology and Socio-cultural change.
2. An overview of Mer social organisation and kinship system.
3. Some crucial aspects of Mer lineage structure.
4. Salient features of Mer kinship organisation.

5. A global analysis of historical and theoretical aspects of cross-cousin marriage.

It is significant to note that the Mers numbered nearly 50,000 in 1951, but in 1981 their strength increased to about 2,00,000. The exact figures could not be ascertained due to restriction on recording caste identities in the information collected by the Census of India. Although I have not dealt with the impact of rising numbers on the Mer Society, I have the feeling that the village organization and the preferential bilateral cross-cousin marriage have been adversely affected. Of course, this calls for a special investigation.

The Mer book of 1961 presents baseline data on ecological, technological and cultural aspects of the Mer region along with the analysis of social organisation and structure. It calls for a review at this point of time, and we shall deal with the subject in a diachronic perspective. While we present an overview of Mer social structure and kinship organisation in the next sections, we shall not touch upon it at this point of time. Here we shall try to link all the available information along with socio-cultural changes in the sub-regions of the Mers, taking the physiographical dimension as the analytical datum.

The Mer region is distinctly characterised by four physiographical features. They are :

(i) The Barda Hills covering about one fifth of the undulating land area ;
(ii) The seven small and medium size rivers falling in the Indian ocean cutting through the coastal ridge-line stretching over fifty miles in length ;
(iii) The little desert of Mokal near the central coastline ; and
(iv) The agricultural belts of highland and lowland areas in the west and the south-east respectively.

These four divisions of the Mer land are slightly differently formulated here than those described in 1961 Mer book The natural resources such as flora, fauna, minerals, etc. and technological developments which can exploit such assets play a significant role in the lives of the people. This is true both in the times of peace and disturbance and also during rapidly changing conditions. We have here kept in focus ecological balance within the geographical conditions to present a brief analysis of socio-cultural changes taking place in the Mer dominated multi-caste villages of the region.

The Barda Hills

The area of Barda Hills is covered with patches of thin desiduous jungle. The main population is of the herdsmen called Rabaris rearing cows, sheep and goats inhabiting 23 *nes* or cluster of straw huts or mud-houses in the hilly tracks. A few small villages on the fringe of the hill area are also inhabited by them. A sprinkle of Mer population is found specially in villages of the fringe area. In the remote past, lions were reported to be found in the interior jungle of Barda Hills. Other wild animals found here are panther, jackal, wolf, etc. The Gujarat Government had proposed to rehabilitate lions here in a planned sanctuary, but it has been dropped now. The herdsmen as well as the Mers occasionally eat meat of fowls, goats, sheep, rabbits and other birds but their staple food consist of cereals and pulses such as *jawar*, *bajara*, rice, gram etc. The interior hill area does not produce adequate quantities of these cereals and pulses. Therefore, the people have to get the domestic needs from nearby plane villages or towns. The wild fruit trees such as *ber*, *rayan*, *karamda*, *ounda* etc. and the mangoes in some select area are found but not enough to support the people. The supply of timber and firewood from the forests is not of much significance. The Rabaris earn their livelihood mainly by selling milk, *ghee*, etc.

The undulating terrain of the hills makes it difficult for the people to take advantage of the flow of technological advancement. The use of radio, tape-recorder and transistor is picking up fast. An Ashram Shala (literally hermit-school) has been recently started where about 100 children of the herdsmen came to take instructions. There is one cement factory, 4 white clay factories and 6 chalk-stick powder factories exploiting natural resources from the foot-hills of Barda, A stretch of sandstone quarries in this area has been an old time industry. Most of these sandstone quarry units are managed by the local entrepreneurs and managed by day-wage labourers. It is natural that there is little change in the lives of the people in the interior of this hilly area of scarce resources. The social organisation and the structural relations between various castes and sub-castes have not changed much. The Rabaris who are largely illiterate, form the dominant caste-group in the area. The electricity has not been extended to the interior hill area, but the frequency of buses on the main tar road via Bileshwar Mahadev temple has increased the visits of pilgrims, specially at the time of the annual fair held there.

It will be clear from the comparative overview of the physiography of other parts of the Mer land in the subsequent paragraphs that it presents a staggering diversity. However, the style of life of most of the well-to-do Mers, including dress, consumer goods, use of bicycles as a mode of casual travel, etc. cut across the diversity found in the entire Mer land. We shall deal with the general uniformity in socio-cultural changes at the end of this descriptive account. We shall also bring out certain contrasting aspects of the social organisation of multi-caste Mer villages and general living conditions of the Mers in conformity with changes spurred by the acceptance of new technology in the following paragraphs.

The Seven Small and Medium River Basins

Out of a total of seven rivers worth the name, three rivers are prominent. River Bhadar flowing from the Central part of the Saurashtra peninsula and passing through this area, is a river of heavy seasonal floods which occur with damaging impact on the life and property every three to four years. It is naturally of great consequence in the south-east part of the lowland area. Similarly, river Ozat has its own impact on the lives of the people. A sizeable area is left unfertile and inhospitable at the mouth of the river due to vast swamps of Bhadar, Ozat and Madhuvanti rivers in the lowland sub-region. These swamps are collectively much larger than the Modhwada and Gangajal swamps of about 4×6 miles formed by rivulets flowing from Barda Hills into the sea through the highland. These areas are good neither for agriculture nor for human or animal habitation. If new technology is able to improve, exploit and reclaim such natural waste-lands, it can became a great boon to the people of these areas.

Of the 58 miles long coastal strip of the Mer region starting from Madhavpur town to Miani village about 10 to 15 miles (16 to 24 kms.) area is rendered useless by creeks and swamp terminals meeting the sea. The rest of it all is inter-spersed by hard sandstone beehive rocks where hardly anything can be grown. The land-side fall of the ridge at places is made up of fertile alluvial soil brought down with river floods. There are about a dozen villages in the vicinity of the ridge on either side of the city of Porbandar which itself is built on the coastal ridge plateau. The villages on the ridge are divided into those belonging to the lowland and highland areas respectively.

The crops raised in the land of villages of the ridge area have undergone radical changes. Formerly all the farmers, i.e. Mers, Kolis and Brahmins were growing pulses, such as *arad*, *mag*, and horse-gram and coarse cereals such as *chins*, *kang*, *bajara*, and *jawar*. With the use of improved seeds, fertilizers, etc. the yield of crops such as ground-nut, *jawar*, *bajara*, and horse-gram has increased considerably. The coarse variety of cereals have been almost eliminated. Fishing activity has been encouraged by the Gujarat Government, but it remains the monopoly of the fisherman and Kharva communities, with a stronghold at the Porbandar city. The Mers and others in general do not make use of abundant fish-wealth in the sea either for domestic consumption or for trade. The Kharvas who were formerly disciplined and well-behaved have become haughty strong and powerful. Although the city is a centre of pilgrimage and the birth-place of Mahatma Gandhi, its crime rate is quite high. The business communities such as Lohana, Bania and Khojas do not have the sole control any more over trade and business as the enterprising educated Mers and others have entered into the field of trade and commerce. Animal husbandry is practised by the Mers and the others as before, and it provides milk and other products for domestic use as well as for selling the same in the market.

The use of new technology such as improving agricultural implements, tools, etc. have been increasing rather more rapidly in the highland and ridge villages than in the lowland. The use of radio and transistors for entertainment and general instruction has been increasing among those who can afford. For commuting and transportation of goods and services, the use of public buses, private taxies and trucks has been the order of the day. A few villages, especially on the highland ridge area have four to five trucks owned by a few well-to-do families of the Mers.

Formerly the houses were of mud-walls and roofs were laid with natural stone-slates laid on wooden rafters or local earthen tiles of several sizes These have been replaced by houses of stones, cement concrete and plastered with cement or lime (*Chuna*), a local product used in house building since long. The roofs are now laid with imported Manglore tiles.

Those who are large land-holders and have wells for lift-irrigation with pump-sets spend most of the fair weather months in the farm-houses, and some of them later return to their ancestral homes in the villages. With the influx of machine made goods, e.g. shoes, stitched clothes, etc. the artisans are deserting the villages and so also the Lohana or Bania shop-keepers going away for earning livelihood in the neighbouring towns and cities. The organisation of credit-cooperative service societies have also affected the business of big shop-keepers. The village *Panchayats* have been active in improving roads, supplying tap water to households and bringing electricity for private and public use, for street lighting, etc. in the villages. In some of the large villages in the ridge area, middle schools or high schools have come up for the education of the young, but those seeking higher education have the facility to study while lodging in the Maher Students Boarding House in Porbandar or commute daily from the villages nearby.

The Tiny Desert Areas

A part of the southern central strip of the Mer region has all the characteristics of a little patch of salt-waste desert where nothing but shrubs grow. This is called the Mokal desert. A large chunk of it is located in the lowland except a narrow strip that enters the highland near Porbandar ridge and goes a little beyond. A couple of villages on the fringe of this desert area are economically weak due to unfertile land and frequent visitation of floods in low lying areas. People here have to earn their living more by practising animal husbandry than agriculture because of the patches of salt-waste lands in the fields. The main occupation of the people therefore remain animal husbandry and labour in sandstone quarries and salt factories.

The Agricultural Belts of Highland and Lowland

The remaining sections of the western highland and south-east lowland provide relatively fertile agricultural belts of the Mer region. The concentration of population is also higher in the villages located in these areas.

The technological vectors have made an impact of great significance on village organisation and socio-cultural change in the highland and the lowland areas having contrasting geographical and ecological conditions. Certain aspects of socio-cultural change due to modernising influences from the outside world are no doubt common. This is especially so with respect to acceptance of innovations and practices of day-to-day relevance. Barring the new features of modernising influences and uniformity in the superficial aspects of life-styles, the distinctive ecological-cum-geographical characteristics have kept the two sub-regions of the Mer land in a position of duality as before.

2

PERSISTENCE OF MARKED DUALITY OF THE SUB-REGIONS

THE fact that technology cannot fully wipe out dichotomy or duality created by physiography is perhaps nowhere more clearly demonstrated than in the Mer region. We shall present a concise account of the impact of technological developments on the social organisation of the multi-caste Mer villages of these two sub-regions under sub-heads, viz. : (i) Transformation of the highland and (ii) Old profile of the lowland.

Before we proceed to do that, it should be noted that social habits and food taboos of the Mers and others have retained ecological balance as far as we can generally observe. The few wild animals such as panthers and jackals found in the foot-hills of Barda were occasionally hunted in the past, specially for the protection of cattle-wealth of the people living in the area. They are no more to be found in large number. The sheep and goats reared by the Rabaris and Bharwads are sometimes used for sacrifice or killing by vagharis to supply meat to the non-vegetarians who do not make more than forty per cent of the population in the area. The meat of fowls or rabbits, fish etc. is also eaten occasionally. The meat of cows and peacocks is taboo to eat on strictly religious ground. The buffaloes are reared mainly for milk supply. The popular trees of edible fruits that remain prominent are mangoes, *papaiya*, *rayan*, and *ber*, etc., while rest of the trees do not yield such fruits but are shady. The most popular trees are tamarind, *banian*, *pipal*, etc. and a variety of bush-trees. The horses were favourite among the Mers but they are now-a-days getting out of vogue due to increasing use of automobiles and bicycles for commuting outside the village. The pack animals such as donkeys and camels are kept by potters and cattle breeders such as Bharwad or Rabari herdsman.

Transformation of the Highland

The highland is popularly called the Barda panthak, it is being flanked on western side by the foot-hills of Barda Hills. As indicated in the Mer book (1961), it is rugged and uneven land area of considerable size. It is spread over by patches of stoney waste-land covered with bushes and shrubs along with sizable plots of agricultural land from village to village. The villages near the coastal area are said to be in the danger of loosing their agricultural land because of salinity spreading fast due to the salt factories operating nearby. The government is planning to implement the scheme of reclamation of salt (*Khar*) land. The richness and depth of the layer of fertile soil are not satisfactory. They vary greatly from place to place, making it essential for the farmers to use ample manure for reaping a good harvest. Formerly, it was not possible for many farmers to raise two crops in winter and summer seasons because the conventional water wells were not so deep and were not able to get assured water supply as today. In the last two decades or so, the State Government has been liberal in advancing subsidy and loans to needy farmers for sinking field-wells deeper so as to assure year round water supply for drinking and irrigation. When most of the prospective farmers had initially dug their field-wells, they were further encouraged to make use of Government subsidy and loans to fix electricity or diesel oil pump-sets for lift-irrigation. This enabled most of the highland farmers to change over to the practice of raising two crops per annum depending upon the size and quality of land-holdings.

In most of the highland villages of large-size with population over 1,000 souls, there are primary schools. In most of villages we can invariably find if not more, atleast one young Mer man who has been trained in elementary mechanical engineering. It has made most villages almost self-sufficient in taking care of mechanical breakdowns or setting up new units of pump-sets, flour mills, etc. anywhere in this area. Hardly any one takes the trouble of using the old time hand-mills for grinding the daily quota of flour to prepare bread for the family. Not only this, the diesel oil flour mills wherever they existed in the villages have been replaced by those run by electric motors, thanks to the spread of electrification to almost all the villages in the highland.

This spread of new technology coupled with increase in the means of communication due to use of bicycles, motor-cycles and public transport etc., the tempo of phyiscal mobility and daily commuting for business or work has greatly increased. All these changes and the changes in cropping pattern have completely transformed the character of the age-old village organisation.

The earlier pattern of raising cereals such as *jawar*, *bajara*, etc. and a variety of pulses, cotton, sugar-cane as suited to local conditions has almost vanished. Now the staple food crops for domestic use are not limited to these careals, rice also has found its place in daily use. The sugarcane and cotton growing, which had increased in the earlier phases of development has given place to ground-nut. This revolution in cropping pattern has made large land-holders fairly rich. The new practice of multiple cropping made possible due to assured well water irrigation and fertilizers has compelled the Mer farmers to shift their households from the villages to the fields. The use of tractors, mechanical crushers and hullers have added to this revolution. The large nucleated villages have now developed a new pattern of dispersed housing units like satellites in the far-flung agricultural land of the village.

The families having small and marginal land-holdings and some of those of artisans and other castes are the only ones to be found living in the ancestral villages all round the year. Many of those who have shifted their families to farm-houses have made their stay there highly comfortable. Some of them have built *pucca* houses and installed fans, sanitary latrines etc. and even got flour mills set up to cater to a complex of neighbouring households living in the fields. This means that the cattle, domestic pets, etc. are kept in the fields. The children going to primary schools or high-schools use bicycles, public bus services or live in hostels during the period of there education.

The situation has so worsened the settlement pattern in the

highland area that the original nucleated village is found deserted by the old-timers and as a result, the vertical solidarity and inter-dependence of the farmers with the artisan castes have been damaged considerably. The age-old system of *jajamani* relationship of food-producing and service castes is thereby greatly weakened. Most of the better off artisan families have left the villages and/or shifted to take up other occupations in nearby or distant towns. There have been cases of traditional barber or potter families switching over the skills of better paid vacations like those of tailor, or carpenter. Similarly some of the black-smiths or gold-smiths have taken to other occupations outside the village. Many educated youths of artisan castes have taken to teaching, clerical or other kinds of semi-skilled jobs wherever available. This process of socio-cultural and occupational changes spurred by the invasion of technological vectors and spread of education on village organisation is shaking up the age-old foundation of village life, which was based on mechanical model. The Brahmin prist and the genealogist Bard who were patronised by the well-to-do Mers have no doubt retained their respect among Mers but the ritual roles that they used to play at the level of the household have been minimised. Some Brahmins who amassed wealth abroad are reported to contribute their might in building school and temples in their villages. Formerly they would not take such a leading role in village life.

Formerly, most people in the highland used to build their own houses by themselves, specially upto walls made up of stone-slates, mud-lining and cow-dung plaster. The roofs, doors, windows, etc. traditionally laid out and artistically carved by carpenters and stone-cutters were the common sight. The old time Mer house was basically a one piece large-room unit with a verandah, main entrance and a small kitchen with a passage from inside the room itself. The new houses now built in the farms or in the villages are more or less prototypes of those of highcastes with a two-room set in a row on the ground floor with a verandah covered by an iron grill, an encloser and the first floor room. A staircase from inside the interior ground floor room leads to the first floor room and terrace if any. The other striking changes is the absence of multi-colour decorative wall designs in mural and clay work in relief made by women, which were at once useful and decorative. Special sheds are now built for cattle and storage or fodder etc. along with dwelling houses in the farm or village.

The old and unused village houses of those living in the farms, by and large remain uncared for in the highland area. Some houses in the villages are however used only occasionally during monsoon or during wedding seasons or at the time of the Holi festival. It is at this time that the youths get the opportunity to play *dandia ras* or other traditional competitive games.

The common barran grass land for grazing the cattle of the villages is partially used for the purpose of community get-together. Some sections of the plots of village land are surplus and are used by the village Panchayat for buliding public structures of warehouses, schools, houses for landless labourers etc. The various taxes levied by the village Panchayat for providing civic amenities such as street-lights, drinking water-taps, etc. are not paid up by the villagers regularly. These tax levies are refused payments by the families residing in farm houses for good. The investment of money collected by way of local taxes, public contribution, donation and loan specially for building overhead water tanks, pipe line etc. have turned out to be serious liabilities in some villages. A few village Panchayats have thus come under debt due to unpaid loans taken for providing infrastructure facilities which have remained incomplete or get damaged beyond repair. It should be pointed out that in contrast to these difficulties and financial liabilities of village Panchayats, the credit cooperative and service societies are reported to be doing well Moreover, the experience of the common people with the lead-bank agents collecting small saving investments and giving loans has also been quite satisfactory in the highland villages.

One of the outstanding features of the village scene in the past was the sight of the village herds of cows and buffaloes collected by every morning after sun-rise by the herdsman called *gaval*. This can hardly be witnessed as a live event now in the highland villages since many families keep their milch cattle and bullocks with them in the farms. The services of the *gavals* being now less in demand, do not fetch assured livelihood to many of them. Therefore, they have taken to other occupations elsewhere and so the hamlets of the people of Rabari or Vaghari castes located on outskirts of villages have been reduced in number. The weaver families and others of the Harijan castes, who worked as agricultural labourers also have either abandoned the village homes or taken to other occupations.

The gossip and leisure-time groups of men who used to assemble at the village *chora* or community house are not to be seen daily except on special occasions of marriages and festivals. The traditional lineage based village leadership is weakening and it is counter-balanced by the elected young leaders. New leaders raised on party lines count heavily on external political forces in power at the taluka and district levels. The ceremonial occasions of marriage etc. are organised by the well-to-do families at the farm houses. This is feasible because transportation of goods and services to the farms in fair weather is no more a serious problem. Most of the large size villages in the highland have atleast four to five families owning trucks in partnership or otherwise. In the villages of Modhwada in the highland for instance, there are reported to be 150 trucks owned by the Mers. It is significant to note that quite a few educated and rich Mers have their bungalow type houses in the city of Porbandar. About fifty per cent of private transportation companies with trucks, taxies or station wagons is reported to be in the hands of the better off Mers. The village of Chhaya, which is now a suburb of Porbandar city provides a unique example of the Mers of many lineages and having unequal socio-economic background living with the people of other communities.

Old Profile of the Lowland

The lowland is called the Gher Panthak, and it seems to have been once a shallow gulf from which sea waters had been pushed back centuries ago by river floods depositing thick layers of alluvial soil from upper streams. If wells are dug in this area, one invariably gets saline water at the depth of 10 to 20 feet. The ground water tanks for storing rain water in the low-lying area are the main sources of drinking water supply in summer. Most of the tanks were specially dug for this purpose by collective manual labour of the villagers and the earth accumulated in the process was used for the purpose of making a low wall or embankment. The tank water collected in the monsoon did not last sufficiently long for the people to get through the summer without creating acute scarcity of water for drinking and washing. The river beds of Bhadar, Ozat and Madhuvanti are sometimes used for scooping holes in the sandy soil to get water in the summer. This facility however, is available mainly in the upper reaches of these rivers.

The land around almost all the thirty five villages in the lowland area remain water-logged in monsoon. The villages built either on higher mounds, coastal ridge or higher peripheral area, look like a tiny island. Besides, they are facing the serious problems of getting safe drinking water, disposal of human and animal waste and of the dead during rainy season. In the last two decades or so, the problem of supplying drinking water to scarcity-hit villages has been solved by putting up main pipe connections from the tube-wells located in the bed of Bhadar river near the town of Kutiana. There are about 20 villages enjoying this kind of facility due to successful application of technological devices to this area since last quarter of the century. More villages are likely to be covered by water services of main pipe line in the near future. The State Government has prepared a scheme to tame the floods of Bhadar river in order to mitigate the hardships of the villages situated in the lowland called Gher Panthak.

The physiographical chararcter of the lowland has given it a kind of levelling uniformity where there is little variety of flora and fauna. Wild variety of bushes, cactus and some trees are to be found on mostly katcha road-sides and around village settlements pitched on high mounds, most of the remaining agricultural fields are almost without big trees. The entire lowlands however become lush green carpet when crops grow in abundance after the monsoon. The crops fail only when flood-waters do not recede in time or when the rains have been scanty in the catchment areas of the rivers.

The monsoon of 1983 turned out to be an event of greatest disaster for this area and its surrounding region. It was indeed a mini-deluge unheard of in the living memory of the people. In certain places, the average rain of the whole year fell with vengeance in two days time. It took more than a month for the floods to recede from all parts. Some villages were entirely washed away along with live-stock and people. Hundreds of people, thousands of cattle and property worth crores got perished. Many survived by living on house roofs, tree-tops, etc. keeping alive for days without food or clean water. Rehabilitation work was started on war footing and a Flood Relief Committee was appointed under the Chairmanship of the former Chief Minister of Gujarat. The city of Porbandar was surrounded by flood waters and since there was no facility for the water to be drained away, a set of high power pump-sets had to be employed to save the people from spread of disease and further destruction of their property. Apart from what is normally destroyed in heavy floods, the usual wealth of fauna to be found here are peacocks, cranes and ducks etc. of the wild variety and migratory birds such as heron. Specially the herons are to be found in the water-logged areas in the vicinity of coastal ridge. People do not kill or eat peacocks and herons on religious ground. The meat eaters among the Mers are in minority, and they generally eat the meat of fawls, goats, etc. in the same way as it is the practice in the highland. On the whole, the ecological balance is not greatly disturbed under normal circumstances.

The cropping pattern in the area has not been radically changed from the past. In the plots on the periphery of sub-murging areas of the lowland, people have been raising more than two crops if well water for irrigation is available. The *jawar* has been the main crop in the area and the farmers usually reap rich harvest with the least efforts put into various agricultural operations. The horse-gram, sugar-cane, wheat, rice and *bajara* crops are raised as usual. Now-a-days, growing cotton has become common in some areas. But those in the higher area who are able to manage irrigation water to take more than two crops, give priority to ground-nut. The improved farm technology including pesticides, fertilizers, tools, etc. are adopted without much reserve, but tractors and such other heavy tools and equipments are not used because of the natural weakness of deep layers of soft soil in the fields. The heavy machines such as tractors cannot but sink down into the soil and may become difficult or impossible to retrieve.

There are no prospects for the development of mining activity here. The sandstones for building houses in the villages have to be imported from distant places in the times of fair weather. The housing pattern in the villages of this area is becoming more and more of closely built units. This is because it is impossible to build houses in the farmland and live there longer and comfortably as in the highland. The village sites on high mounds are extended by reclaiming peripheral land where cattle refuge is dumped for building houses there after some years. The process of getting more land for the growing housing demand is thus painfully slow. The cement concrete building technique has been adopted in some villages by the well-to-do farmers. The latest technique of durable building material is employed especially for laying a solid foundation of the house in a relatively low-lying area of the village site. The plans of such new houses are generally the imitations of the high caste houses. The latest housing pattern remains the same as reported in the case of highland area.

The position of artisans in the lowland is relatively better on account of the village organisation remaining more or less intact. The rise of population and spread of education in the members of their households have no doubt led to migration of young boys of artisans outside the village. However, their usual services have remained indispensable and the elements of old time *jajmani* relationships have retained the vertical solidarity of various castes at the village level. The services of the temple priest, other Brahmins and Barets have not been greatly damaged. The town of Kutiana, formerly a Muslim stronghold, and the border of lowland has turned out to be a centre of organising religious discourses and celebrations of Ramayan Saptah, etc. where the people of the highland villages often pay visits quite in large number.

The agricultural labourers here are in great demand. The plots of surplus land of the village site have been distributed to landless labourers for their dwellings in many lowland villages. The village Panchayats have obviously taken liberal attitude towards helping the scheduled castes as well as artisan households practising agricultural labour in building houses of their own. Most of these houses are comfortable to live in except during monsoon when unexpected flood comes in.

3

COMPARISON AND CONTRAST BETWEEN SUB-REGIONS WITH REGARD TO SOCIO-CULTURAL CHANGE SPURRED BY NEW TECHNOLOGY

IN this chapter, we shall deal with the impact of overall changes in the socio-cultural life of the Mers. It is interesting to note that certain changes have become inevitable because of the impact of demographic changes and technological revolution. The Mers have nearly doubled in population in the last 30 years or so. The ever increasing number of people in the villages of highland and the lowland areas have created adverse impact on the character of village organisation. This is one of the reasons of dispersal of village population in the highland besides adoption of new farm technology. The general innovative attitude of the people is at its greatest height. The new technology has no doubt become a sort of levelling agents of change for both the sub-regions but has not become very significant in surmounting the basic differences of the physiography of the highland and the lowland areas. It will be useful to indicate briefly some points of contrast between these two sub-regions in the following analysis.

(1) The highland Mers have found that the investment in adopting technological innovations in agriculture is rewarding. As reported earlier, a large number of private taxi, truck and tractor owners are found in the highland. Some of the lowland Mers who are large land-holders, can easily invest more money in farm technology but the physiographical condition of their habitat does not permit it. This is why there is an emphasis by the people of lowland on the maintenance of cattle for milk, ploughing and other purposes. The cows and bullocks are highly priced for their continuing positive role in giving milk

and providing animal power for agriculture. The buffaloes are equally valued for milk, and sometimes they may be yoked to the plough. The horses have more or less got out of favour both in lowland and highland due to greater use of automobiles.

In the highland, the animal labour for agriculture has been considerably replaced by machine power as compared to the position in the lowland. The herdsmen (*gaval*) families here are breaking up and some of their male members have taken to labour or have deserted the villages for working elsewhere to earn their bread. On the other hand, *gaval* remains an important unit of service in multi-caste village organisation of the lowland. In some of the large villages there, one may find two sets of cattle herds, one for tending cows and the other for buffaloes. In contrast to this, the mechanisation of farm technology in the highland has made the services of the herdsmen nearly unessential. The mechanisation of agriculture has made the dispersal of residential houses to the farms inevitable. The old time village circulation system was suitable for bullock-carts to pass by, and the tractors cannot be parked easily in the village. Besides, it is costly too to commute to village and leave farm equipments without personal care.

(2) In a normal year, when the rainfall and seasonal conditions are satisfactory, the people in the lowland area are economically better off. The spare time and money of the well-to-do farmers is generally spent away organising *bhajan* mandalies and other pastimes such as drinking, gambling etc. However, some of the enterprising rich and educated Mers have begun to invest surplus time and money in starting a variety of small scale industries. In the towns of Kutiani and Ranavav, one finds four cotton ginning mills, five oil pressing mills etc. About 30 per cent of the Mer entrepreneurs are reported to be engaged in the management of these industries. In recent times a few of them have established small business firms in other urban centres including Porbandar. Incidentally, it is the only town in the highland and largest in the Mer region as a whole.

The lowland Mers however are attracted towards the District towns of Junagadh. There are some Mer dominated villages in Vanthali, Keshod, Malia, Manavadar, Mangrol, Mandarna and Junagadh talukas known for their prosperity. It may be noted that all parts of these talukas do not fall in lowland. One of the most respected Mer religious leaders Shri Mahant Vijayadasji, the former Minister for Agriculture in the State, and now the President of the Gujarat Pradesh Congress (I) Committee hails from the village of Dhandhusar near Junagadh. He exercises powerful influence on the Mers of the lowland, and has achieved the distinction of being elected unopposed from Ranavav constituency in the legislative assembly of the State.

(3) The spread of education among the Mers of highland was in the past greater as compared with that in the lowland. A boarding house for the Mer students has now come into existence in Junagadh. The highland Mers had however a historical advantage of having the first Maher Students Boarding House in Porbandar established by late—Shri Maldevbhai Keshwara. It is here that most of the first batch of educated Mer leaders grew up as students. The former president of the Gujarat Pradesh Congress (I) Committee, late Shri Maldevji Odedara was one of the harbingers of this movement among the Mers.

Some of the first generation foreign going Mers also came from the highland villages. Late Sheth Manji Kalidas known as the King of Sugar Industry in Uganda (Africa) helped many Mers in realising their ambitions and spirit of adventure. Even today, a large proportion of Mer families settled in foreign countries come from the highland villages. The most outstanding of them is Shri Jethabhai Visana, Bar-at-law, residing in England.

(4) The advantage of rural electrification after Independence came first to the highland where it became instantly useful in the improvement of agricultural practices. It was easier to lay down electric-poles, assembly lines, sub-stations, etc. in the highland than in the lowland area because of risky nature of the terrain there. After the supply of electric connections, the electric power was quickly used by the clients in the highland villages. All the flour-mills owned by private persons or cooperative societies in the highland are being run now with the

help of electric motors. The highlanders in principle seems to have declared moratorium on the use of the outdated diesel oil machines vis-a-vis those run with the help of electric power. But they did not altogether say good-bye to diesel oil machines and pump-sets because of the problem of staggering and uncertainty of the electric supply for agricultural and industrial use. It has been the policy of the government that if electricity is not used for the purpose of agricultural development, it cannot be provided on priority bases to any section of rural areas. Initially, priority was naturally accorded in the lowland, but withheld because geographical and ecological conditions did not guarantee optimum utilisation of electricity for agriculture. However, the people decided to develop cottage industries in rural areas, and so the rules had to be relaxed. Electricity has now become a need based priority infrastructure in the development of both agriculture and small-scale industries in the Mer region.

In recent years, a liberal policy has been adopted by the government and the network of electricity is being laid in the lowland. But nature seems to be working against the interest of these people as there are frequent visitation of heavy floods or cyclones in this area. These forces of nature cause immense damage to electric poles and installations every now and then. The villages in central part of the lowland specially suffer more from the lack of regular electricity supply due to these providential reasons. Nevertheless, there are quite a few villages in relatively higher boarder areas of lowland where electricity lines can and have been laid. But the people of some of these villages are so poor that they have found it difficult to raise enough matching contributions necessary to meet foundational cost of rural electrifications.

(5) The wind of overall socio-cultural change is clearly spreading over the Mer region as in other parts of Gujarat. The distinguishing cultural symbols between the Mers and other ethnic groups are no more respected. The desire of retaining ones identity of sub-castes is weakening day-by-day among the people of both the sub-regions of the Mer land. The dress of the younger generation—man and children—of all castes and communities consists of pants, bush-shirt, sari, skirt,

blouse, frocks etc. which are specially stitched or got ready-made in the market. This change has largely brought about the kind of leveling effect and apparant similarity on the visual picture of Mers and others.

Mer women have shown the tendency to continue to wear some traditional attires and symbols in personal effects. This is specially discernible in the case of women living in villages. Some educated young Mer women though have fully changed over to the dress and ornaments of the high-caste women. Other women most of whom work on the farms have retained traditional dress with some modifications in design, use of textile material, etc.

The Mer males have taken to high-caste dress more rapidly than the females. They have nearly given up wearing huge turbans of white cloth on the head. Similarly, they have given up the short-cut tunic called *angadi* and replaced it by shirt or bush-shirt. The baggy trouser called ***chorne*** is no doubt retained, but with considerable modification and economy in the cloth used in stitching.

(6) The traditional weapons of war-fare among the Mers were axe (*kuhadi*), sword, spear (*bhala*), etc. They were beautifully designed by the village blacksmith. An axe or a spear was invariably held in hand by a young Mer man. Some would also carry a gun with them while travelling from ones own village to another village. Of these weapons of war, the former varities are no more carried publicly for protection or as the prestige symbol. The traditional ornaments of gold, silver and glass beads etc. are getting out of vogue from daily use, but they are still worn at the time of marriage and during other festive occasions. Relatively speaking. the tendency of retaining cultural symbols. values and behavioural pattern seems to be stronger among the Mers of lowland than those of the highland. It is the working Mer women in either of the sub-regions who still promote traditional symbols of Mer culture as much as feasible.

(7) In the bygone days. an outsider male member, young or old. would not dare to enter a village without covering his head. This was a strict code of conduct to be complied with by the Mers themselves, as compared to the man of other higher

castes, especially those coming from urban areas. Today hardly anyone takes a serious view of infringement of this etiquette and other rules of discipline both among men and women. Nevertheless, no one would like to go out of the way to affront the honour and respectability of young and old Mer women. One may find quite a few young men wearing ultra modern pants, bush-shirts, etc. working in the fields, on machines and automobiles in the highland as well as lowland sub-regions. The educated youngmen are generally influenced by the city fashions in both the sub-regions of the Mer land.

(8) The religious life of the Mers in both the sub-regions has become richer than before, though the attendance at the annual fair of Madhavpur has not been looked upon now as a matter of great prestige by the young. Going to see the movies has become more fashionable instead. The existing temples of worship and shrines are being renovated by contributions of the public in general or by special groups, and some new ones are under construction. The beliefs in superstition and ancestor worship are as much in vogue as before. The worship of Ram Deo Pir and Vachhada Dada have been refined, sublimated and elaborated in the fashion of Sanskritic deities. A new religious cult or Brahmakumari from outside the Mer land seems to be making inroads into the highland, while the influence of the Kabir Sampradaya continues to be as powerful as before, specially among the Mers of the lowland.

4

AN OVERVIEW OF MER SOCIETY AND KINSHIP ORGANISATION

BEFORE presenting an overview of the structural relationships among the Mers, we may generalise that the societies practising simpler occupations and relatively less exploitative division of labour among its population, can manage their affairs with relatively homogeneous structural relationships in social and economic activities. On the other hand, the societies having complex division of labour cannot do so without relatively heterogeneous social structure and organisation.

Keeping such a broad comparative stance in mind, we may subsume that relatively simpler tribal societies with nomadic past are likely to present contrast and dichotomy of structural relationships involving consanguine groups on the one hand and affinal groups on the other. As opposed to this, the settled peasant societies having more developed technology and complex division of labour are likely to have evolved some kind of trichotomous social structures which result from constant merger of the aforesaid bi-polar structural relationships primarily based on descent and marital status.

An omnidirectional or double descent society having patrilineal and matrilineal or mixed mode of inheritance gives rise to complex relationship and impermanent groupings of kin folk. The Mer Society, broadly speaking is a fairly developed socio-cultural entity. Its patrilineal descent groups and social organisation are complex, elaborate and pervasive. The elements of stability and durability in the social structure of the Mer society are of unique nature.

The Mers from a strictly endogamous descent group in each of the unilineal fourteen patrilineages where each male member is the potential founder of a branch or segment of the original lineage.* Each large size lineage in general is made up of scattered sub-groups of families divided into maximal lineages, major segments. minor segments and minimal lineages. The living or dead male heads of each of them are independent and all powerful in their sub-groups of procreation. All the Mer lineages and their respective segments remain meaningful structural units due to common interests of their members having fundamental rights in land. Similarly, they remain significant in the control of marriages of members of the sub-groups concerned. A Mer patrilineage being an exogamous ethnic group, all the members are brothers and sisters and are called *bhandarana* in relation to one another. The *bhandarana* as a group do not intermarry as they are generally the members of a common patrilineage. The members of other patrilineages are eligible for marriage and are called *natarian*.

The obligation of mutual assistance locally called *dhal*, also play a significant role in the solidarity of lineage segments or subsegments which were formed in the remote past. Today these solidary groups are found to reside in one or more villages founded by the founder ancestor of a segment or its part. However, on account of preferential bilateral or symmetrical cross-cousin marriage, the females came from more than one *nataria (marriageable)* lineages as wives and weaken the solidarity subsumed between the members of patrilineages. The situation of interpenetration of women by marriage between groups of people of marriageable lineages or segments mitigates chances of Mer lineages or their parts waging groups war with one another. For a lineage as a whole or its part has no inherent enmity except sometimes between families. This is another factor which gives rise to a unique position of strength to each Mer male member as a potential head of a family or that of a future segment. This unconscious, sub-conscious or cognitive identity of omnipotence felt by a male member possibly prompts him to take law in hand, so to say, and to fight his

* It may be noted that matrilineages are not highly segmented as patrilineages are, because the dual mode of residence of the males is generally associated with them. Similar situation prevails in cognatic, double or omnidirectional descent systems,[1]

rival in land or woman without restraint. In this process, he may kill or be killed by his opponent who may be anybody, even his uterine brother.

The origin and perpetuation of blood-feuds which were practised by the Mers in the recent past seems to lay in this kind of value loaded and culturally conditioned behaviour arising from their social structure and organisation. The tendency to wage blood feud is no doubt gradually weakening amongst the educated Mers today. But the tendency to ignore legal rational norms of the court of law has not fully vanished. The tendency to settle scores by violence against crime committed due to insult or injustice or deprivation of personal property by the opponent, persists. And, the origin of it as indicated earlier, lies more in the structure of patrilineages than in the Mer kinship organisation. As said before, it gives omnipotence to a young Mer male descendant who, by all means, is a potential head of segment of his lineage for all practical purposes. Any unwanted advice or interference in his personal affairs by the father or even an elder brother may not easily submit a man to change his point of view and position regarding a social or economic problem of long standing or of day-to-day significance. He has a tendency to remain adament and stick to his guns on serious matters of dispute.

In historical perspective, a Mer male had little respect for the legal rational system of law courts of the Mughal or British origin. This kind of attitude arose possibly on account of the sense of individual omnipotence of the Mer man referred to earlier, and also because in the past the Mughal and British political agents had tried to subdue the "sovereignty" of the Mers in their homeland. In theory, the continuity of criminal tendency among the Mers, even today, has its origin in the turbulent history. They have sacrificed precious lives as the price to protect their homeland *(bhom)* against the enemies and are "legitimately proud" of it. It seems that the macro-level geo-political conflicts for suprimacy over the land are gradually transferred to meso and micro level feuds of inter-lineage and intra-lineage groups of the Mers.

The other explanatory theory behind the phenomenon of feuds among the Mers is based on paradigm from the science of human biology called "territorial instinct". Under the normal circumstances, the instinct to possess, exploit and control ones land of birth is common to all primates as to human beings. The craving for land leads to clashes between narrower range of kins or wider range of consanguines or non-kins. The conflicts for the control of ones habitat in general has been an age-old phenomenon. Such behavioural pattern has become a norm common to most living creatures in a region. The modern phenomenon of imposing restrictions and controls over land, sea and outer space by different nations of the world is a manifestation of the same kind.

If my impressions are not wrong, atleast for the last 30 years or more, the nuclear families among the Mers have as a rule out-numbered joint families. And, according to the findings of the statistical sample survey of 1981-1982 conducted by me in 12 villages of the Mers, the percentage of nuclear families among the Mers was 74.00% and correspondingly, the percentage of joint families was 26.00%.[2] At the back of this nearly constant normative pattern of the composition of the Mer household, there seems to lie the hold of the system of unilineal male descent among the Mers, and also that of inheritance of property in the male line. The Mer kinship organisation has been superimposed by the inherent subconscious superiority of the male. The Mer male is thus a symbol, so to say, of the cognitive inheritance of Mer family culture. The usual pattern of residence after marriage is obviously virilocal rather than uxorilocal except where Mer man moves to the wife's village when he inherits his father-in-law's property in absence of a son to the latter. If such a man has more than one son, the couple's uxorilocal residence causes dispersal of the male members of the family only spatially not substantially.

A nuclear family among the Mers generally retain social ties intact with the joint family. A young man rearing his nuclear family is usually given separate room or space for building a house from the joint family accommodation or house site. He is also given a part of ancestral land for self-cultivation. His name is recorded in the government land record of rights at a later stage.

It is likely that rights in ancestral property may not be

shared equally by all sons while the parents are alive. Most of the sons in a joint family are in intimate touch with the family of mother's brother or father's sister due to the custom of preferential cross-cousin marriage. Thus extreme form of attachment to the patrilineal hard-core descent group, i.e. joint family, is softened in respect of interpersonal relationships with the patrilineage of mother's brother where father's sister is married. A person sometimes behaves in a contradictory manner towards the consanguines and affines, depending on good or bad relationship in actual practice rather than the ideal pattern. A man and his sister preferring to marry other marriageable woman and her brother respectively, are involved in sister exchange. In the next generation, the sons on either side may marry such woman who is ones mother's brother's daughter. And the daughters on the either side may marry their father's sister's sons. This kind of marital relationships are not as a rule found to be repeated often among the Mers, but sometimes they do take place.

The cross-cousin marriage among the Mers acts as an ingenious device of resolving conflicts in the society because a woman can share membership of her natal patrilineage with her daughter's children if her brother's son marries the latter. Otherwise, it is possible that the bonds between brother and sister get weakened. It is also possible that consanguanity and affinity bonds go on intertwining between those families who prefer mechanical model and enter into the ideal pattern of bilateral cross-cousin marriage from generation to generation. Naturally, it can strengthen social bonds between the wife giver and wife receiver, and thereby the bonds between brother and sister remain intact. This means that inter-lineage solidary cuts across intra-lineage solidarity among the Mers under ideal pattern of kinship organisation.

The practice of divorce by either sex is being easy in principle, although reported to be lesser in vogue today. The problem of fixing the identity of children by sociological or biological paternity is not required to be solved so long as they are babies and are not separated from wife and sent quickly to the divorced husband for good. Sometimes a widow remarries a younger kinsman of her dead husband and bears children by him, and she regards her new husband as sociological father of these children. This can be called a kind of widow inheritance. It happens to be a kind of fabrication of kinship ties of the actual rather than the ideal relationship. It should be noted that the use of kinship terms of address and reference between the parties concerned undergoes changes due to such events. The Mer kinship terms are sometimes extended to non-kins in the community or in the society outside the Mer fold. Naturally, this practice gives rise to pseudo or quasi-kinship relationships especially with the persons of other castes, ethnic groups or communities as the case may be.

REFERENCES

1. It is suggested here to refer to the *Encyclopaedia Britanica*, 1964, No. 13, pp. 403-05, for necessary support.
2. Harshad R. Trivedi, *A Survey of Social and Educational Status of the Mers*, unpublished report submitted to the Gujarat Backward Class Board, Gandhinagar, 1982 ; Institute of Cultural and Urban Anthropology, Ahmedabad.

5

SOME CRUCIAL ASPECTS OF MER LINEAGE STRUCTURE

THE origins of the Mer lineages have been attributed to superhuman ancestors and to natural phenomena of mythological fame, such as sun, moon and fire. The structure of a particular Mer lineage is linked with one of non-historical lines of descent noted above. This is a common phenomenon among most ethnic groups in India, and the Mers are no exception. Remote conceptualization and reconstruction of the structure of Mer lineages in the distant historical past may therefore be looked upon as pseudo-history.[1] The remote history of most of the ethnic groups in many ancient societies has the same characteristics.

Lineage structure has been the backbone of the Mer social system. Important aspects of this are presented in the following paragraphs explaining conceptual and theoretical issues involved in the analysis of structural relationships.

(1) The affective formal unit in the social system of the Mers was and continues to be the joint family and at the time of marriage, two joint families come together and forge intimate affinal ties. This affinal solidarity between two families counter balances respective lineage solidarity of the families concerned.

(2) Once two families from highland and lowland Mers are related by marriages between their respective family members, the bonds of marriage, ideally speaking, are further strengthened in the subsequent generations due to the custom of bilateral or symmetrical cross-cousin marriage.

(3) The affinal ties by marriage of the members of two families sometimes narrow down the circle of intimate relationships to such an extent that the people may not know much

about all the members of their own lineage living in distant villages.

(4) Almost all the Mer dominated villages in the recent past acted as nucleus of social relationships having narrow circles of affinal ties spread out in neighbouring villages. And, these circles of *affinal villages* as well as *kin villages* overlap or intersperse one another in such a way that they virtually unite all the Mer villages by the network of affinal and kinship ties. This phenomenon is cogently illustrated below.

(5) In the Mer book of 1961, I have presented the Conjunctural Reconstruction Chart[2] of affinal ties between two or three or four lineages extending upto the full circle of all the 14 lineages. It was discussed with different informants and was approved by them. The macro circle, so to say, of 14 lineages has been shown in the web of marriage ties representing the ideal or *mechanical model* of structural relationships.* The other circles of 2, 3 and 4 lineages linked with affinal ties give a reliable assessment of the meso and micro level profiles of the hard-core social structure providing ample scope of evolving a *statistical model.* It means that at the time of my first field work, these three types of inter-lineage marriages predominated. However, it does not give any idea of the percentages of actual occurrence of these circles of marital relationships at that point of time.

(6) On account of rapid communication facilities today, a Mer family is virtually free to choose marriage partners for their children from distant villages. But in the past, a family was largely found to prefer cross-cousins for marriage of children only from neighbouring villages for practical reasons. If the affines are living close by, they can be of mutual assis-

* As Levi-Strauss puts it, "Fundamentally, the sole difference between prescriptive marriage and preferential marriage is at the level of model. It corresponds to the difference which I have since proposed between what I call a "mechanical model" and a 'statistical model", i.e. in case, a model the elements of which are on the same scale as the things whose relationships it defines : the classes, lineages, degrees ; while in the other case, the model must be abstracted from significant factors underlying distributions which are apparently regulated in terms of probabilities."[3]

tance (called *dhal*) in agricultural operations or at the time of emergency.

(7) Irrespective of lineage difference, every Mer speaks proudly of the virtuous, brave and pious men or women born in the community and looks upon them as "brother" or "sister" as the case may be. This brings about a kind of moral solidarity among all the Mers or different descent groups living in any part of India or abroad.

(8) The genealogies of Mer lineages are recorded in the books of the hereditary bards or genealogists tracing descent from male members who wield supreme power in conducting the affairs of a lineage, because, marriage is patrilocal. A woman after marriage is separated from the natal familiy and village and so the males by and large play more prominent role than females in performing religious rites, rituals, deciding inheritance of property, etc. and in the daily walk of life.

(9) The Mer women who were well versed in the traditional skills and arts of wall painting, clay-work, spinning, patchwork, etc. got distributed among other lineages by marriages. It is said that the elements of artistic skills of decorating dwelling houses developed by the women of the highland villages (i.e. four lineages) spread to lowland villages (i.e. ten lineages)* and vice-versa due to wife giving and wife receiving practices between the families spread over the whole of the Mer region.[4] Today these artistic traditions of wall painting and relief work in clay, are on the verge of extinction, and this cherished cultural attribute is nearly dissociated from the traditional virtues of a desirable Mer bride. Similarly, the armamental tattoo marks on the body of a newly wed girl are no more insisted upon or appreciated as in the past.

(10) The names of women from different lineages who are married in the same village are likely to have identical names. They have to be distinguished. And therefore, they are recognised by the names of their fathers and their lineages.

* (i). The highland four lineages are Keshwara, Odedara, Shisodia and Rajshakha.

(ii). The lowland ten lineages are Parmar, Solanki, Chauhan, Chudasama, Bhatti, Jadeja, Chavada, Vadher, Vala and Vaghela.

This is because in the case of divorce, a woman's identity has to be re-linked to her natal family and village, so that her eligibility for any other *nataria* lineage is determined. This is why the genealogist of a Mer family would write the name of the father of a married woman after her name, in her husband's family genealogy.

(11) At the level of the conjugal family or minimal lineage of her husband, a woman is likely to be possessed by the deities and spirits of her natal village or family. And the members of her conjugal family would, as and when require, try their best to appease these super-human elements of her natal family or lineage. This and the previous point indicates that in the past, there existed a positive moral influence, pressure and social impact of a woman's natal lineage on the conjugal lineage and village.

(12) The solidarity of the whole maximal lineage may obviously suffer a setback because of the feeling of cognitive omnipotence felt by the Males. And, as said before it is inherited from the lineage structure built around the form of patrilocal residence. All or most of the members of maximal lineage are not usually found assembling on the same day and at a particular shrine of a lineage deity for worship. In recent times this has changed considerably. And at the time of renovation or laying down the new foundation of the shrine of a lineage deity many members came forward to give donations and participate in organising various activities of the function.

(13) The members of all the fourteen lineages no doubt get a chance every year to meet at the religious fair held at the coastal town of Madhavpur in the lowland area. Now-a-days, the educated Mers do not go out of the way to visit this fair. Those who have time and means to do so and are tradition bound take full advantage of enjoying this as well as other fairs where some members of many a Mer lineage get-together. Sometimes sporadic brawls and fights take place at such public fairs between rival groups of Mers or other groups due to insults or jokes exchanged between individuals prone to make public exhibition of the feeling of their omnipotence. This kind of behavioural pattern seems to be inherent in the psyche of the Mers as perhaps in many other ethnic groups of

Saurashtra.

(14) Each of the families or minor segments of a Mer lineage found in a village shows solidarity and strength with regard to economic, ritual and jural pursuits. But if the number of such segments was very large, say, around 20 instead of 10 joint or extended families in a village, it was likely that the lineage solidarity in the village suffered a setback. This happened because in certain villages the groups of such minor segments insisted upon having their own community halls called *chora* for the members to get-together and discuss their own problems. An instance of a special case of this kind was to be found in the Odedar village which had as many as 24 such *choras*. It is difficult to say whether all their community houses in Odedar are functionally useful today.

(15) Serious quarrels flared up among paternal cousins if someone seduced the wife of the other. Not only this, even if a man wanted to marry the divorced wife of a fellow-lineage member in the same village, he was not permitted to do so directly. This becomes possible only then when the divorced woman concerned firstly married a member of another lineage in a different village (1st stage). And, only after obtaining the divorce from the latter she became eligible for remarriage (2nd stage) with the chosen close kinsman of her first husband in the same village or minor segment.

(16) The genealogy of the Khistri village, which represent a major segment of Gohdania Mers of Sisodia lineage revealed the following interesting facts from the long chart presented in the Mer book of 1961

(i) the village headman (patel) was supposed to know by memory the names of male and female ancestors atleast upto 8 and 5 generations respectively ;

(ii) the right of traditional headsmanship went either to the eldest or youngest son of the previous headman, specially, in alternate order from one generation to the other ;

(iii) a great-grand-son of a person was named after the name of his great-grand-father ; and

(iv) a person (specially a headman) took the privilege

of marrying as many as eight wives when he failed to get a male descendant from previous wives.

In the end, it should be noted that when husband and wife are not cross-cousins they are looked upon as such in ideal terms. On account of such implications, parents on either side of the couple are treated as putative mother's brother and father's sister respectively. And when this putative relationship is taken in practical life as real, the lineage of the two individuals stand on equal footing. Therefore, the parents-in-law on either side are treated as if they are related by kinship in this limited context only.

REFERENCES

1. Harshad R. Trivedi, *Mers of Saurashtra,* Faculty of Arts, M.S. University of Baroda, 1961, p. 41.
2. *Ibid,* p. 37.
3. Strauss, Claude Levi, *The Elimentary Structures of Kinship,* translated from French by James H. Bell, John R. Strumer and Rodney Needham, Eyre & Spottiswood, London, 1967, p. XXXV.
4. Trivedi, H.R., *op. cit.,* p. 40.

6

THEORETICAL ISSUES AND INTRAGROUP PERSPECTIVE OF MER KINSHIP ORGANISATION

In this chapter, we shall deal with the salient features of Mer kinship organisation. As presented in the following paragraphs, these features are grouped under two sub-themes, viz. :

(i) Conceptual and theoretical issues of cross-cousin marriage ; and

(ii) Intra-group relations and taboos.

Conceptual and Theoretical Issues

We shall try here to delineate *emic* and *etic* aspects of Mer kinship organisation along with the application of Levi-Strauss's *mechanical model* and *statistical model* for the analysis of cross-cousin marriage among the Mers. The analysis has been made as exhaustive and as elaborate as possible so as to throw new light on the subject for the benefit of scholars.

1. The structural relationship among the Mers have positive correlation to social status by age of a person within the scale of generations in the total social system. Every individual attains three time-bound positions in life, i.e. childhood, adulthood and old age and when a person passes on from the first stage to the second, or from the second to the third one, his status changes accordingly. The terms of address, behaviour and personal relations with the people of ones own generation are generally those of equality in all respects. In comparison to generation-group, age-group in the past was not of much significance in the use of kinship terminology and maintenance of structural relationships. For instance, a middle aged man would call a young boy uncle or *kaka* if he falls in the category of his father's generation inspite of a big gap between their ages

due to late birth of one of them. In exceptional circumstances, when the younger paternal uncle realise that he is just a boy and his paternal cousin is much older in age, he sets aside his superiority in terms of status by generation-group and calls him brother instead of son. This means that the *emic* point of view established by tradition, is abandoned in the favour of *etic* point of view as soon as it is found to be fallacious in practice and does not match with the reality of life.

2. There is a well-known proverb among the Mers, viz.: *fui pachhad bhatriji*, which means that a female paternal cousin follows a maternal aunt by way of marriage to the latter's son. This means that it is obligatory to marry ones daughter to ones sister's son. It likewise implies that ones sister's daughter is preferred for marriage with ones own son. For, it happens frequently that a person marries his sister's husband's sister by way of sister exchange.

3. Although it has been customary for a man to take the sister's daughter in marriage for his own son, it is sub-consciously understood as an act of exchange or *satun* in local language.* Thus, the immigration of a girl after marriage to ones mother's brother's son is equivalent to exchange. The word *satun* or exchange conveys a situation of bargain.[1] This kind of bargain in terms of social relationships from the insider's (*emic*) point of view, is not looked upon as an act of superiority on either side. The Mers believe that it is more charitable, generous and ethical on the part of a man to give his daughter in marriage to his sister's son without expecting her daughter to be returned in marriage for his son. This *mechanical model* (positive) of bilateral cross-cousin marriage system was talked about by a traditional Mer man as a matter of great pride and valour. Thus the cognitive significance of cross-cousin marriage by *satun* is "inferior" to the one way traffic of *fui pachhad*

* One of Mer friends, a senior government officer, in Ahmedabad, remarked that they do not use the word *satun* to express this kind of relationship. He further said that in an endogamous caste where there is scarcity of daughters, the interested parties have to exchange brides for marrying their sons. And, it is this that is called exchange or *satun* in matrimonial alliance. The term *satun* has been used in my Mer book of 1961 in the context in which it is used here.

bhatriji as said before. In other words, a matrilateral cross-cousin marriage, or a symmetrical marriage of the daughter of a man to his sister's sons is of higher social value and significance to the Mers than the patrilateral cross-cousin marriage where a man expects his sister's daughter to marry his own son. This means that even though preferential cross-cousin marriage regulation allows a person to bring his sister's daughter in marriage for his son, he may not go in for it, in case he can get the daughter of his wife's brother or some one not related in any other way. Thus, the *mechanical model* of symmetrical cross-cousin marriage has two dimensions, one negative and other positive, so to say. The negative dimension refers to not so respectable a preference of marrying ones son to sister's daughter (as in *satun*) while the "positive dimension" refers to perfectly respectable preference to marry ones son to ones wife's brother's daughter (as in *fui pachhad bhatriji*).

4. The form of bilateral cross-cousin marriage as it was in practice in the past among the Mers has remained consistent with regard to the use of kinship terms of address and reference in the sense that relatively little differentiation was to be felt between the *mechanical model* and *statistical model* in the Mer marriage system. In general, a couple was compelled to give latitude to the obligation of preferential cross-cousins for marriage of the children if their opposite number was devoid of marriageable son or daughter as the case may be.

5. As indicated in the special chart of an extended family-tree in the Mer book (1961), the most common types of unions by marriage were :[3]

(i) A man married to his mother's brother's daughter,
(ii) A man married to father's sister's daughter,
(iii) A man married to father's father's brother's daughter's daughter,
(iv) A man married to mother's father's brother's sister's daughter, and lastly,
(v) A man married to father's father's brother's daughter's son's daughter.

The above categories of "cross-cousin marriages" within

the range of five generations were perhaps accounted for by higher percentage of occurrence in the past. The junior sororate and levirate unions were certainly not reported to be so common.

6. Whenever sororatic unions occur, two sisters become co-wives of a person and they become step-mothers to each other's children. When two unrelated women marry one man, they are looked upon as putative sisters. In either case, their relations may not be cordial. However, when a woman dies leaving young children, her younger sister if available is preferred to replace her by marriage for practical reasons eventhough she may not always prove to be affectionate towards her elder sister's growing children. The leviratic unions are preferred only when the problem of division and inheritance of ancestral property by the widow of a man or the children is not desired due to several reasons. If two sisters are married to two brothers and if the elder brother happens to die young, it was possible theoretically for the widow to marry the younger brother of her dead husband and thereby become the co-wife of her sister. The leviratic union would get merged in this way into sororatic. one. In reality, the widow is not forced to accept such a union. She is free to remarry any one else whether she has children or not. But if she choses to do so, she has to face the discomfort arising out of the sororatic-cum-leviratic unions. The discomfort remains in store because such unions may lead to strained relationship particularly because it creates a strange complex of step-children and step-mother relationship around uterine sisters.

7. With regard to the use of kinship terminology involved in symmetrical cross-cousin marriage, Dumont rightly observes that the Mers oppose collectively parallel and cross relatives in Ego's generation respectively, i.e. *bhandarna* (consanguines) and *natarian* (affines). "Actually, for uncles and aunts they use four of its names arranged in an unorthodox way to distinguish two couples of uncles and aunts : those comprehending a parallel relative (FB and FBW, MSH and MS : *kaka* and *mosi*) and those comprehending a cross relative (FSH and FS, MB and MBW ; *mamo* and *fui*)."[3] This carries the influence of *mechanical model* of cross-cousin marriage with a difference. But there

seems to be no room for the use of other more prevalent Gujarati or Northern Indian types of kinship terminology eventhough the style of cross-cousin marriage may be totally ignored in a particular case. It may be noted that when two strange families enter into matrimonial alliance, the differences of lineage origin between certain categories of relatives are blurred and the *mechanical model* of the marriage system fictitiously converts certain affines into consanguines and vice-versa. This may be called the cognitive extension of the meaning of aparently mundane aspects of cross-cousin marriage into the realm of lineage organisation.

8. The relations between ones wife and sister in a Mer family generally remain cordial, because it is likely that they may have to exchange their children for the purpose of marriage as per the rule of preferential cross-cousin marriage. In contrast to this, the wives of two real brothers may easily come in conflict, because each one may have vested interest in the management and property of the joint family to which their husbands belong. If they are not on good terms, they may accelerate the fission of the joint family. The conflicts between mother-in-law and daughter-in-law also cost the unity or jointness of the family. But when the daughter-in-law is the daughter of mother's brother as in *fui pachhad bhatriji* their relations are as cordial as those between daughter and mother. In the case where the mother-in-law and daughter-in-law come from two affinal lineage, the unity of joint family may be endangered, if they are not on good terms. This means that the members of two opposing lineages as in the case cited above may work either for unity or division of a family. It shows that the *mechanical model* behaviour can have no edge over the devient behaviour of individuals in the favour of an emerging *statistical model.*

9. The three parts of affinal relationships favourite among the Mers are : (1) Mother's brother and sister's son (*mamo-bhanej*), (2) wife's brother and sister's husband (*salo-banevi*) and (3) husbands of two real sisters (*sadhu bhai*).[4] The bonds of *mamo-bhanej* are generally intimate and durable, those between *salo-banevi* are flexible due to the implied scope of divorce between a person's sister and her husband, and those of *sadhu*

bhai are said to be generally sound, because, eventhough the two may not be real brothers, they are looked upon as belonging to the same lineage fictitiously in the context of *mechanical model* of bilateral cross-cousin marriage. In general, the ideal social relationship between the pairs of kins or affines carry a variety of cognitive meanings and interpretations of structural significance as indicated above.

10. The role of genealogist or *vahivancha* in the lineage structure and kinship organisation of the Mers is highly significant. The genealogists tour Mer village and record the names of the new-borne sons and daughters in the genealogical books (*chopada*) maintained by them.[5] They visit the villages of their hosts after a couple of years, or also when invited by a family on special occasions. The names of the women married in the family are also listed in the genealogy of her husband's family. However, as indicated earlier, care is taken to see that the name of her father along with that of his lineage and village is also registered. In the first electoral list of the voters prepared after Independence of India, the Government had printed the husband's name and surname after the name of a married Mer woman. This was resented upon by the Mers mainly because they permit divorce of a woman through a written agreement (*lakhanu*) with the consent of both the parties. Therefore, they desired that in principle it is not proper to tie down in a government document a woman's name for good to her first husband. For, it is essential to see that her desire for remarriage with another man in future is not jeopardised in any way. This *emic* point of view stemming as it does from the established norms of the Mer lineage structure naturally gives a feeling of confrontation to the government establishment in charge of organising adult franchise for democratic voting. In the end, however, it is the *etic* point that was allowed to prevail by educated Mers in the larger interest of maintaining uniformity in the procedure and process of preparing voters' list for general elections.

Intra-group Kinship Relations

It is the thesis of this writer that :

> "The organisation of a society practising bilateral cross-cousin marriage represents, so to say, a kind of cyclical form of human relationship giving facility to other unrelated groups of people, having similar lineal descent. to get in but not to get out of its tentacles except under special circumstances."

We may now elaborate the statement throwing light on the issues arising out of intragroup kinship relations and related taboos. This is done by providing some illustrations in support of the above thesis.

1. The detailed study of the Mer lineages have revealed that some branch lineages of various Rajput clans entered into matrimonial relationships with the original Mers of Keshwara and perhaps the Odedara, Khunti or Rajshakha lineages. Before entering into the Mer social organisation, these Rajput groups practised matrilateral asymmetrical cross-cousin marriage, i.e. marriage with the mother's brother's daughter only. It is plausible that subsequently when they entered into matrimonial relations with the Mers, they allowed themselves to be governed by the kinship organisation of the Mers permitting bilateral cross-cousin marriage which allowed marriage of a person not only with mother's brother's daughter but also with father's sister's daughter. It is reported that Mer type of bilateral cross-cousin marriages are possible also among the Kathi Darbar, Rajputs and Ahirs of Saurashtra but not among other categoriesof Rajputs

2. As a matter of fact, when the general category of Rajput groups or families mixed up with the Mers, they had to succumb automatically to the structural and organisational norms of the Mer society and get merged therein for ever. This is understandable, because the children of Rajput man by a Mer woman are customarily expected to become the preferential mates of the children of either sex of their Mer maternal uncle. While on the other hand, the son of a paternal uncle cannot think of marrying the daughter of paternal aunt who follow Rajput way of kinship relationships permitting only matrilateral cross-cousin marriage and not patrilateral one. This is obvious-

ly because the latter type of marriage is permitted among the Mers but prohibited among the Rajputs.

3. The Rajputs who had no chance to win the love of the Mer women or who did not like to mix up with the Mers, might have looked upon these "proselytised" Rajputs as low ; because they might have argued, as they do today, that to marry ones father's sister's daughter amounts to *satun* which is not looked upon as respectable. The Brahmanical models of incest, prohibiting marriage with the blood relations upto 5 generations on mother's side, and 7 generations on the father's side seem to have been kept in mind by the Rajputs.

Thus, the Rajputs consider it as good as incest if they have to marry close blood relative such as father's sister's daughter. By disliking and rejecting this kind of relationship, the Rajputs claim themselves to be a step superior to those who decided to enter into the social organisation of the Mers. These ideas of superiority and inferiority are only relative and cannot be treated as substantive elements in wider context of human relationships. As a habit, the members of one caste look down upon the members of another caste as low if the latter do not observe the principles of incest or similar other taboos such as ritual cleanliness, etc. accepted by them. This is probably the reason why the Rajput men who once married Mer women, got permanently merged into the Mer social fold and could not in fact escape from the web of Mer kinship organisation and lineage structure. In their downward social mobility, in the light of Brahmanical *emic* point of view, so to say, leading to the socalled "backward" social organisation of the Mers, some of the Rajputs were probably compelled by the circumstances to have a permanent settlement with the Mer community. It is possible that the concept of *satun* in the case of patrilateral cross-cousin marriage among the Mers is shared by the people of Rajput Mer lineages.

4. In support of the obvious and rightful claim of the Mers, that some groups of Rajputs merged with them, an illustration is cited. It is mentioned that the Jethva prince, Randhiraji, married a Mer woman, called Pabibai and so he preferred to remain in the Mer fold at the cost of his right to

ascend to the throne of Porbandar state. He voluntarily abdicated his right to rule and passed on the chieftainship of the Porbandar State to his younger brother. Randhiraji's descendants are now known as the Rajshakha Mers. The term Rajshakha means those descended from the royal branch. The Rajshakha Mers are also called Khunti Mers after the village of Khuntwad which was gifted away to Pabibai by her father, and where she was born.

5. It is important to note that the Mers of Ajmer Merwara and Madhya Pradesh areas are reported not to permit marriage with the father's sister's daughter like other Rajputs on the ground of incest. These Mers seem to have been proselytised, so to say, in the reverse direction, by the Rajputs with whom they had come in contact as a weaker minority group. It is a case which may be looked upon as an instance of upward social mobility. In fact, the Mers of Ajmer Merwara and Madhya Pradesh areas have changed to such an extent that reportedly they do not allow junior sororate, junior levirate or even either kind of cross-cousin marriage. However, if a person commits breach of the customary law by violating any of these prohibition, the caste elders may fine him, but do not go to the extent of excommunicating him. The fact that such violations are tolerated, shows that these Mers wish to retain their identity inspite of being converted to the Rajput model of marriage rules.

6. There is another important social issue which is directly associated with the kinship organisation of the Mers. It is a fact that the Mers of Saurashtra did not practice in the past the custom of female infanticide as other Rajputs did. Here a legitimate question comes up to mind as to why did not the Mers practice female infanticide specially when they claim themselves to be Rajputs ? This question obviously represents an *etic* point of view. A satisfactory answer to it is to be found in the differences in kinship organisation of the Mers and the Rajputs as explained in the following illustrations.

It has been said that the Jadeja Rajputs of the former Jamnagar State lodged a complaint against the British civic law of the then Rajsthanik Court prohibiting female infanticide. They are reported to have forwarded the argument that they practice the custom because they did not like to offer their sisters or daughters to other ethnic groups in marriage during the times of scarcity of grooms in their own endogamous group. This is because they believed that to handover one's sister or daughter for marriage to an alien group in the absence of a match in ones own marriageable group is to invite the greatest abuse and humiliation on the family and the whole caste As a matter of fact, many Rajputs are reported to have taken daughters for raising progeny from the lower caste groups other than Rajputs and to uphold their pride and prestige. But they have retained dignity by not giving daughters to others rated lower to them

7. The Mer kinship organisation permitting bilateral cross-cousin marriage is such that it is theoretically possible even for two lineages alone to carry on for generations together, matrimonial relations between them without looking for brides from other ethnic groups elsewhere. To be specific, the children of two marriageable (*nataria*) families can theoretically go on marrying their children and even great-grand-children of opposite sexes among themselves, and the process may go on upto the 9th generation without any break, provided of course, there is no dearth of marriageable children on either side. It means that in theory, the principle of "bifurcated merging" of the affines may never come to an end. Thus, the question of practising female infanticide on the ground of dearth of brides or grooms, and of the problems of upholding social prestige and ethnic pride of the group can hardly crop up among the people practising the Mer type of kinship system.

8. There is another important point of general interest which refers to settling cases of inheritance of property in the context of Mer kinship organisation. The point is that in the case of bilateral system of cross-cousin marriage, when a brother and a sister decide to marry their children to each other's children of either sex according to the rules of preferential mating, the couple that has sons benefits most by importing daughters from the other side. If either of these two couples happens to die sonless, having one or two daughters married as per the rule, it is likely that the property of the deceased sonless couple may be inherited by the daughters married in the sister's

or the brother's family as the case may be. This means that the ancestral property of the Mers remain with the Mer community itself and cannot be annexed to the state or the ruling power under normal circumstances.

REFERENCES

1. Trivedi, H.R., *op. cit.*, p. 58.
2. *Ibid*, p. 57.
3. Dumont, Louis, "Marriage in India : Present State of the Question", *Contributions to Indian Sociology*, No. 9, December 1966, p. 103.
4. Trivedi, H.R., *op. cit.*, p. 62.
5, *Ibid*, p. 40.

7

REGIONAL PERSPECTIVE OF MER KINSHIP ORGANISATION AND SOCIO-ECONOMIC CHANGE

In this chapter, we shall throw light on the position of bilateral cross-cousin marriage in the neighbouring regions along with the impact of socio-cultural change on the Mer kinship organisation. The following paragraphs are grouped under distinct headings to make the analysis of the theme meaningful.

The Position in Neighbouring Regions

Here we shall examine in brief some regional variations of the kinship system of the Mers and other communities particularly in the neighbouring states.

1. Among the Hindus in northern India, "the marriage regulations are based mainly on the consideration of consanguinity,[1] the marriage between near cousins is viewed as incestuous union. The Mers of Saurashtra provide one of the striking exceptions to this rule. But the Mers of Ajmer Merwada and Madhya Pradesh area as reported earlier, avoid cross-cousin of either side for marriage purpose.[2]
2. The kinship terminology prevalent in Central India (central zone) as described by Irawati Karve is identical with the northern terminology. But because certain castes of the "central zone" practice asymmetrical cross-cousin marriage with mother's brother's daughter only, the term *mame* or *mama* for mother's brother is used also for the wife's father besides the usual northern term *sosara*.[3] It is interesting to note here that though the Mers of Saurashtra belong to the "central zone"

they agree much more with some people of "Southern zone" who practice symmetrical or bilateral cross-cousin marriage.[4]

3. The Mers of Saurashtra differ, so to say, with certain people of South India in one important respect, viz. that they do not practice marriage of a man with his elder sister's daughter as some of the latter do.[5]
4. The Mer term *mama* is identical with the similar term *mava* in Kannada terminology. But the Mers do not have a special prefix like the Sanskritic word "Sahodar" to be used before *mava* which refers only to uterine mother's brother.[6]
5. While trying to assess the patterns of marriage and kinship organisation in Gujarat, Iravati Karve found it difficult to get a correct picture of the situation. Specific difficulties arose in the case of Koli, Dhed and Bhil tribe regarding prevalence of cross-cousin marriage. She was, it seems, given contradictory response, probably because of variation in the marriage norms of their sub-castes. Some allowed marriage with mother's brother's daughter while others flatly refused the prevalence of the custom.[7] According to G.S. Ghurye, the people of Saurashtra allow marriages between cousins in the forth generation. The prevalence of marriage with ones maternal uncle's daughter was however reported to be a practice obligatory among certain groups of people.[8] This appears to have been endorsed by Furer Heimendorf in a general remark where he says, "conversations with Indian colleagues and students from Northern India have, on the whole, confirmed my view that the tendency to the formation of relatively small endogamous units is by no means confined to Southern India."[9]
6. The study of marriage and kinship of the Gangadikara Vokkaligas of Mysore, by Bhavani Banerjee throws interesting light on the prevalence of cross-cousin marriage in that community. The matrilateral cross-cousin marriage was said to be more in vogue than the patrilateral one, and the ratio of occurrence between the

two varities was 2:1 and also it was more in favour of mother's brother's daughters. A man would give greater preference to marry mother's brother's daughter than father's sister's daughter. Moreover, the mother's elder son is more often an appropriate candidate for a girl than mother's brother's son. The Mers of Saurashtra follow the same pattern of matrimonial relationship, although these groups do not seem to have prior histroical connections. The absence of earlier contacts between the two is probably reflected in the fact that among Vokkaligas a man marries his elder sister's daughter to the tune of 15% cases of marriages while among the Mers it is totally absent.[10]

7. As referred to earlier, Dumont has made candid remarks in regional context on some aspects of Mer Kinship Terminology, while writing on "Marriage in India" in 1966. He says, "The Mers use four different words for uncles and aunts arranged in an unorthodox way to distinguish two pairs of couples who comprehend parallel relatives in one case and cross relatives in the other case. "Although the words are different, we are here back to Dravidian form, including the fact that the names of two spouses are radically different. To my mind the instances is indicative of the existence in North India of underlying tendencies of South Indian type.[11] Here Dumont implies that the South Indian type of kinship relationships have had some influence in the Northern areas. But if we consider the historical background of the Mers, this implication does not hold water, because the original ancestors of the Mers are said to have come to India from Central Asia. Dumont's hypothesis may be invalidated if it is found that some peasants in Central Asia were culturally similar to the Mers and practised or still retain the Mer type of kinship organisation permitting bilateral cross-cousin marriage.*

* It may be partinent to compare Dumont's appreciation of the book on the Mers with comments of M.S.A. Rao published in 1962 in a review article, where he remarked that "The study is ethnographically poor and theoretically weak".[12] The discerning scholars aware of

I should like to quote here the statement of Kathleen Gough Aberle, for what it is worth. In her recent monograph, entitled *Dravidian Kinship and Modes of Production*, she writes, "I think we have to abandon the nation that there is one single mental pattern underlying all or most of the present and recent Dravidian Kinship systems, expressed in a common terminology, I think that there once was such a pattern. but that proliferation occurred as a result of such processes as state-formation. Aryan and perhaps other immigration, adaptation to different ecological niches, occupations, and positions in the class structure, the evolution of different modes of production and perhaps also the survival or absorption of pre-Dravidian as well as post-Dravidian structures. The numerous present day systems are not reducible to a common set of mental constructs, even though most of them have retained bilateral cross-cousin marriage and some of the terminological equations appropriate to that."[13]

What we learn from Kathleen Gough's analysis is that we should keep our mind open while trying to interpret the patterns of kinship organisation and consider their association with varying socio-economic conditions of the people in historical perspective.

Impact of Socio-economic Change

When a Mer family attains a higher status in the economic, educational, political and occupational areas of life, it develops usually a sense of differentiation with other closely related families in the society. As a result of this, discontinuities arise between the two marriageable lineage groups. This happens specially in relation to their potential relationships governed by preferential symmetrical cross-cousin mating that may take place between the members of opposite seed.

In recent times, the insistence on preferential cross-cousin marriage among the Mers is becoming less and less obligatory

---

Dumont's remarks cited above, as well as the reviews of my book by A.C. Mayer in *Man* (62 : 164 : 1962), and by Joan P. Mencher in *American Anthropologist* (62 : 1962) would clearly find that the comments of Rao on my study of the Mers were hasty and uncalled for.

than before. In some cases, cross-cousin marriage is said to be flatly rejected as a custom of the past and neglected especially by the educated young persons concerned. One of the reasons of this kind of change taking place has been that the marriage system in the past was associated with the practice of child marriage. This practice is now prohibited and is punishable under the Child Marriage Prohibition Act implemented by the Government. Secondly, even when child marriages are made under cover at present, they are not always sure to be successful at a later age when the young partners may happen to dislike each other for various reasons. This can happen even if they may be real cross-cousins.

Similarly, when one of the families becomes economically poor or rich, and when one of the partners is well educated and other not so educated, the differentiation tend to weaken old as well as new marital bonds. This leads to divorce of the couple and as a result, discard ensues between their parents who may or may not be uterine brother and sister. Such a discard naturally continues for a long time or for the whole life. Any sensible sibling would ill-afford to put up with such a discard. Therefore, now-a-days when preferential cross-cousin marriages take place, they are relatively late marriages with the consent of the boy and the girl concerned. The reasons of decline in the incidences of divorce reported among the younger couples these days are said to be lying in this kind of practically viable new style of preferential cross-cousin marriage with the consent of the bride and the groom.

Although the traditional mode of cross-cousin marriage is reported to be on the decline, the kinship terminology classifying cross relatives such as, mother's brother and father-in-law by the same term *mama* is used with due respect as in the past. It means that the *mechanical model* of Mer kinship organisation as reflected in terms of address and reference has remained alive in the minds of the Mers in general. But as preferential cross-cousin marriages are gradually going out of vogue, the kinship terms and marriage system represent a weaker *statistical model.*[13a]* This kind of differentiation

* It is significant to note that the Rabari women from Barda Hills,

between the ideal and the real pattern of cross-cousin marriages is taking place under the impact of the fast changing economic, educational, political and occupational infrastructures on the Mer society. This gives rise to non-archaic pattern free of *mechanical* design in marriage alliances.

In terms of physicalistic realities, each one of these "infrastructures" giving new scales to social life, work like a glass-prism scattering the beam of cross-cousin marrriage relationships from different angles into several hues creating a rainbow of kinship network. By the kinship network, I mean a variety of marriage alliances and counter-alliance as between the members of all the Mer lineages. It is clear at present that the possibility of getting greater number of Mer lineages involved into marriage alliance is increasing. It indicates a new direction in which further enquiries can be made to get realistic insights into the subject. Irrespective of certain elements of unity, equality and opposition in the social structure of the Mers, a kind of succession of affinity and veiled opposition in consanguinity is likely to occur due to reasons of economic inequality between families.

The above analysis shows the possibility of widening the circles of affinal relationships between 14 Mer lineages which in the past might have been occurring much frequently only between proximate and narrower limits and numbers of lineages as shown in the middle section of the Conjectural Reconstruction Chart in the Mer book (1961) referred to before. In any case, the present Mer kinship organisation shows the tendency

Gir Forest and Alach area in Saurashtra address their mother-in-law and father-in-law as *fui* and *mama* respectively. This is inspite of the fact that matrilateral cross-cousin marriage is no more practised among them. It can be explained as a survival of the custom, of bilateral cross-cousin marriage prevalent in that community in the past. The unpublished Ph.D. thesis (in Gujarati) of Asha S. Solanki throws more light on this subject. As indicated earlier, the two other ethnic groups in Saurashtra among whom bilateral cross-cous in marriages are said to be practised even today are Kathi Darbar who are Rajputs and Ahirs who are peasants. The South Gujarat tribal communities of the Gamit and the Warli, as well as some schuduled castes groups including some Bhangis in other parts of Gujarat are reported to practise the custom of bilateral cross-cousin marriage, towards mobility ; and it is movig in the direction of widening its span of horizontal solidarity between all the lineages. This seems to have become possible due to *de facto* liberation attained by the families from the compulsions of preferential cross-cousin marriage at this point in Mer society. The *mechanical model* of cross-cousin marriage had earlier given birth to a number of adventitious dual meso and micro level kinship structures in repetitive patterns of cross-cousin alliances between limited numbers of two, three or four exogamous lineages from generation to generation. But this is no more the case today and the Mer social system is increasingly becoming more and more liberal and therefore complex.

In ideal terms, at the macro level of social organisation, all the fourteen lineages of the Mers can be linked by affinal bonds but at the meso and micro levels, more than four and less than that number of lineages are actually involved in affinal bonds. It seems possible that in changing times of today, frequency of affinal ties tend to shift to macro level lineage bonds than meso or micro level ties. This is an important subject for further investigation.

While discussing matrilateral cross-cousin marriage, Edmund Leach throws interesting light on the subject. He says, "Levi Strauss recognises that the difficulties in the way of maintaining such a system of "circulating connubium" for any length of time must be very considerable and he claims that, in practice, marriage circles will always break down into hierarchies such that the inter-marrying lineages will be of different status. The resulting marriage system would then be hypergamous with the groups at the top receiving women as tribute from their social inferiors."[14] It may be remarked here that such a phenomenon does not occur in the case where bilateral cross-cousin marriage is the rule. This is demonstrated in the case of the Mers. The very idea of hypergamous rules of marriage sound hollow in secieties following bilateral cross-cousin marriage. Such a society can retain egalitarian ethos without being primitive or modern.

Whether hypergamous rules of marriage persist or not, the idea of opposition remain inherent in the case of inter-marrying groups of different ethnic orientations. Since the patrilineal descent system among the Mers is being aided by the bilateral cross-cousin marriage, it amounts to the weakening of structural opposition between the marriageable *natarian* families as well as their lineages. The symbolic or actual acts of opposition are harmonised by the facility of two-way traffic of women by what may be called "exchange". It forms a safety-valve to the exhibition of aggression between those who are wife-giver or wife-receiver. And, it seems that such a subdued aggression worked in reverse gear among the Mers and found an outlet within the patrilineage in the form of blood feuds at the levels of intra-minimal or maximal lineages themselves. This means that the control of external aggression on the Mer society poses a threat to its internal peace and harmony, leading to intra-lineage blood feuds or homicide. Thus, the latent petty quarrels and serious fights are being systematically internalised at the micro-levels of the family and the minimal lineage. In the bygone days these potentialities were clearly demonstrated at the time of annual Holi festival among the Mers. The village youths would divide themselves into two opposing groups and would fight for supremacy when the sacred Holi pot (*kumbha*) is taken round the village. This practice has now got almost out of vogue, otherwise, the heads of many of the youths on each side could be hit.[15] In the past, blood drenched youths had to be literally lifted to their homes for treatment at the end of such mock-fight. However, there was hardly any ill-will persisting between the families of the minimal Mer lineage involved in such symbolic combats.*

* A comparable phenemenon of combats has been reported from the Tsimshin myths on the native theory of marriage of a prince and a princess i.e., father's sister's son and mother's brother's daughter. Opposition between the parties of the two was expressed thus, "when the prince and the princess have married the tribe of the young man's uncle mobilise. Then the tribe of the young woman's uncle mobilise and they have a fight. The two parties cast stones at each other, the heads of many of these of each side are hit. The scares made by the stones on the head of each chief's people are signs of the marriage pledge."[16] This is a descriptive account of implications of the custom of cross-cousin marriage prevalent in an ancient society of the North-West Pecific Coast.

REFERENCES

1. Karve, Irawati, *Kinship Organisation in India*, Asia, Bombay, 1953, p. 117.
2. This information was supplied to me by Shri Jagdishchandra R. Mer who came from Rajputana but who lived in Baroda when the study was done in 1951-54.
3. Karve, Irawati, *op. cit.*, p. 151 ; see also H.R. Trivedi : "Some Aspects of Kinship Terminology Among the Mers of Saurashtra", *Journal of the MS University of Baroda*, 1954, Vol. III, No. 1, p. 163.
4. The analogy of kinship system with some South Indian types should not lead us to the conclusion that all the Mera might have come from South India. For, their history says that some of them who earlier came to Saurashtra are possibly immigrants from Central Asia. It would be much more interesting to know whether any peasant society of Central Asia continued to follow the Mer type of kinship system in the recent past.
5. Karve, Irawati, *op. cit.*, pp. 220-221.
6. Sriniwas, M.N., *Marriage and Family in Mysore*, Bombay, 1942, p. 47. "Such a situation must have arisen after Kannada Society was in contact with Sanskritic culture, for, the term borrowed to express the distinction is a Sanskritic word."
7. Karve, Irawati, *op. cit.*, 3rd edition, 1968, p. 174.
8. Ghurye, G.S., *Family and Kin in Indo-European Culture*, Popular, Bombay, 1962 (2nd Ed.), p. 254.
9. Heimendorf, Christopher Von Furer—"Comment", *Contributions to Indian Sociology*, No. VII, March 1964, p. 101.
10. Banerjee, Bhavani, *Kinship and Marriage of the Gangadikara Vekkaligas of Mysore*, Deccan College, Poona, 1966, p. 84.
11. Dumont, Louis, *op. cit.*, p. 103.
12. Rao, M.S.A., "Analytical Field Work in Sociology", *The Economic Weekly*, Bombay, January 20, 1962, p. 73.
13. Gough, Aberle, Kathleen, *Dravidian Kinship and Modes of Production*, Indian Council of Social Science Research, New Delhi, 1978, pp. 2-3, Irawati Karve Memorial Lecture.

13.a Solanki, Asha S., *Gir, Barda ane Alechna Rabario*, unpublished Ph.D. thesis in Gujarati, The Gujarat University, Ahmedabad, 1975, p. 295.

14. Leach, Edmund, *Levi-Strauss*, Fontana, Collins, 1973, p. 109.
15. Trivedi, H.R., *The Mers of Saurashtra : An Exposition of their Social Structure and Organisation*, M.S. University of Baroda, 1961, p. 36.
16. Leach, Edmund, Ed., *The Structural Study of Myth and Totemism*, Tavistock, London, 1967, p. 26.

8

HISTORICAL AND THEORETICAL DIMENSIONS OF CROSS-COUSIN MARRIAGE, IMPACT OF CHANGE AND FUTURISTIC VIEW OF MER SOCIETY

IN this chapter, we shall first present useful references and theoretical perspectives based on world literature on cross-cousin marriage. Then onwards, we shall proceed to make hypothetical statements on the origins of matrilateral, patrilateral and bilateral cross-cousin marriages, whatever their worth. This will be followed by two special sections dealing with :

(i) normative rules of cross-cousin marriage and dynamic changes among the Mers, and
(ii) futuristic view of the Mer Society and socio-cultural change over time.

In terms of global historical perspective, quite a few theoretical propositions have come to light on the origin and spread of cross-cousin marriage in various parts of the world. The history of the classificatory system of social relationships and dual organisations have been linked with cross-cousin marriage. They have been adequately dealt with in the classical book of W.H.R. Rivers edited by W.J. Perry, 1932. As discussed by Rivers, dual social organisation was found to exist in Malanesia and Australia with cross-cousin marriage. In Africa on the other hand, cross-cousin marriage was to be found in the absence of dual organisation, but it is reported to have been originated due to the influence of some people of North East Africa.[1] Secondly, cross-cousin marriage is said to be the consequence of the transition of a social system from mother-right to father-right. For instance, "In mother right, a man's property goes to his sister's child, but when the change to father-right took place, property would pass to his children, and it has been supposed that the conflict with vested interests was avoided by a marriage in which a man kept inheritance, to some extent atleast in the old channel by marrying his sister's son who was the former inheritor under mother-right, to his daugther."[2] In Terres Island and Malanesia two different kinds of asymmetrical cross-cousin marriages of matrilateral and patrilateral types respectively existed. Rivers further notes that in Australia, cross-cousin marriages were the only ones that existed and generally speaking other forms did not exist. The origin of dual organisations according to him is to be found in the fusion of different ethic groups in marital bonds rather than the fission of one group as such. And that was by and large the order of the day as far as one can imagine. The detailed history of marriage regulations traced by Rivers (in Chapter V, 1932) is not directly relevant here. We shall however make use of what W.J. Perry, the editor of River's book (and author of *Children of the Sun*) has said on the distribution of cross-cousin marriage and dual organisation all over the world (see Appendix III, 1932). Right from India, Indonesia, Oceania, North America, Malanesia, New Guinea, Hobrides Islands, Samea, Australia etc., the dual organisation representing the basic social side of civilization has been the main characteristic of archaic world with Egypt at the centre of all civilizations. The nature of dual social organisation has been composite in the sense that it contains "a duality af territory together with the duality of ruling groups, the two dualities apparently having little to do with each other."[3]

The duality of the ruling groups as distinct from commoners, possibly involved the people concerned into incestuous unions. Intermarriages took place between such people and the other branches of the ruling group itself. "We have a certain amount of evidence to show that the cross-cousin marriage was a feature of this early ruling group. The evidence is particularly clear in the case of the Bugi states of the Southern Colobes, where both tradition and the early genealogical tables of the ruling families show that the cross-çousin marriage was the rule."[4]

Citing instances of marriages in the Old Testament between near kins and sometimes with other migratory ruling groups, Perry says, "it is possible to understand how the ruling groups of the communities of archaic civilization came to institute marriages between relatives as the proper form of marriage throughout the community. They considered it essential to marry kin, and their followers acquired similar ideas. In the cases where the ruling group consisted of two inter-marrying families, it follows that cross-cousins marriage would be universal with the dual organisation."[5]

The Indo-Aryans from the ruling class of the Mahabharata times followed bilateral cross-cousin marriage. As discussed by Ghurye, "There is ample evidence in the lives of a large number of individuals belonging to the famous sanctified families of the Pandavas and Yadavas as represented by the household of Krishna particularly—some of which was discussed by great orthodox writers indicating that they preferred to marry their mother's brother's daughters. I have referred to the much discussed text of the *Satapatha Brahmana* which in its traditional explanation sanctions the marriage of the children of a brother and a sister. A rather obscure passage from the Rigveda, which is a "khila" or an additional hymn, is generally interpreted to refer to the marriage of a person with his mother's brother's or father's daughter as a privilege to which he is entitled. Baudhayan in his *Dharmasutra* however mentions as one of the customs peculiar to the south the marriage of a person with his mother's brother's or father's sister's son."[6] Ghurye further shows in the same text that in the later period, the custom was looked down upon, possibly due to Brahmanical influence.

Coming back to the analysis of Perry, we should note what Levi-Strauss remarks on the evolution of cross-cousin marriage. He shows that Perry does not explain anything new than his fore-runners Morgan and Tylor who identified cross-cousin marriage "simply as a residue of exogamous customs and dual organisation."[7] Levi-Strauss further comments that, "what should have been done, on the contrary, was to treat cross-cousin marriage, rules of exogamy and dual organisation as so many examples of one basic structure." He does not explain what "basic structure" could be. However, he is convinced that "of the three types of insitutions, cross-cousin marriage is the most significant, making the analysis of this form of marriage the veritable *experimentum crucis* in the study of marriage prohibitions."[8] Levi-Strauss is not happy with the suggestion of Swanten who thinks that the origin of cross-cousin marriage "is to be found in a desire to keep the most valuable possession in the family." He seems to be in general agreement with the statement of Louis which says, "cross-cousin marriage is in all probabilities not a phenomenon that has evolved from a single cause but one that has independently arisen in sevral centres for diverse motives."[9]

I wish to give here some hypothetical propositions on the subject. A number of diverse motives for the origin of cross-cousin marriage with regard to (i) matrilateral, (ii) patrilateral or (iii) bilateral varieties have no doubt come to light from various sources. Documentary evidences in this matter can be unearthed by scholars, but in the absence of such studies, it is possible to arrive at a tentative classification of certain behavioural motives underlying the "origins" of cross-cousin marriages in the archaic societies in different parts of the world. With the limited knowldge and scanty reference material at my disposal, I shall briefly present my views on the subject in the following points throwing light on four-fold classifications of the motives as the origins of cross-cousin marriage. It should be noted that Robin Fox has to some extent dealt with this subject without isolaling certain causal dominant factors.[10] However, the subject needs further clarification. I have tried to specify them in the following points. But the order in which I have listed them below, does not signify precedence or succession of the origins of this unique socio-cultural phenomenon.

Hypotheses on Origins of Cross-cousin Marriage

1. *Social Dimension*

There seems to be no doubt that social relationships are substained on account of incest taboos and related prohibition on gratification of sex lying at the rest of survival of human species. It is appropriate to link incest taboos with group exogamy, specially in the case of relatively primitive of simpler societies having developed elementary form of family. The cross-cousin marriage of either of the three varieties are possible in such societies viz. : matrilateral, patrilateral and bilateral one.

2. *Political Dimension*

Pastoral or hunting activities sometimes brought unknown groups of people or families in conflict situations. The cross-cousin marriage involving the practice of wife-giving and wife-receiving may have been a beginning of ending the short or long term hostilities arising out of the socalled right to use land or local resources. Truce in the place of hostility may lead to dual organisations in the form of quasi-political power groups living at a point of time in harmony. If the groups are used to patrilineal descent, it is likely that the patrilateral cross-cousin marriages may predominate over matrilateral and vice-versa, along with or without bilateral cross-cousin alliances.

3. *Economic Dimension*

Relatively settled groups of people having a fairly developed material culture and a keen sense of property rights (in political context) would not likely to loose what they have. Among such groups cross-cousin marriages might have been preferred and such arrangements are likely to have been associated with transition of a group from mother-right to father-right type of social organisation vis-a-vis those of opposing groups. Matrilateral cross-cousin marriages are likely to be predominant over other two forms in the cases of this kind.

4. *Demographic Dimension*

It seems appropriate to think that reduction in the size of population of an ethnic group might lead to cross-cousin marriage alliances. Sudden demise of a number of persons in a group due to disease, accidents, hunting expeditions, fights, etc. can create such a demographic profiles which may lead an endogamous group to resort to cross-cousin marriage for perpetuation of the group. The origins of any one of the basic three varieties of cross-cousin marriages are likely to take place undere such trying circumstances, specially when an endogamous group is reduced to a microscopic minority.

Normative Rules of Cross-cousin Marriage and Dynamic Changes among the Mers

What is not recognised significant in the serious discussions on the subject of kinship organisation in general is perhaps the existence of latent as well as manifest "normative rules" that try to govern actual social relationships between individuals and groups, in a society. In a modern changing society "normative rules" are flexible and affect wider social system, because, they are the outcome of interpenetration of elements of *mechanical model* and *statistical model* in the society. In this sense, a *mechanical model* being an ideal construct, and *statistical model* representing mostly empirical social realities, tend to loose dichotomous stance of their own making. Thus, the "normative rules" of social relationships which are subjected by force of circumstances to absorb changes from time to time, assume altogether new and strange characteristics. Under such pressures of the interpenetration of social elements between the two polar situations of accepting or rejecting the norms of preferential cross-cousin marriage, the "normative rules" force the social reality to be transformed into a third kind of social system model. At the end, a pattern of trichotomous structural relationships may come to life, and the social system may assume subtle dynamic character of organic relationships, lending it a complex functional character. Until this kind of equilibrium is sometimes disturbed by the impact of further more powerful elements, the system is likely to continue to function indefinitely. This is only an ideal position, and the equilibrium model may remain a short lived phenomenon of unstable social situation at a point of time.

At this stage, I should like to point out that Nutini has given elaborate reasons to show that bifurcation of any social reality is not possible in the strict sense of the term. As a corollary to the same, one might also denounce the theory of trichotomy suggested above. Nevertheless, I have conceptualised the trichotomous situation only as a dynamic position wherein there are likely to be many dimensions of dichotomy, and so also of trichotomy of constantly changing social situations under varying conditions and circumstances through which a society today has to pass.[11]

Discussing the subject in his work on elementary structures of kinship at length, Levi-Strauss says, "the general direction which Louis gave to the study of kinship problems was right that exogamy as a regulating principle, stripped of its historical and local modalities, is always likely to follow two different courses in its action, firstly confusing direction and collateral lines, and secondly confusing generations. It is in the same spirit that attention must be paid to a third structural orientation, not limited to exogamy through a necessary concomitant of it, and found also in great number of system without clan and dual organisation. We mean the distinction between collaterals of the same degree, according as kinship is established through a relative of the same or different sex."[12]

It is interesting to reflect on the Mer social situation in this context. Rapidly changing life situations among the Mers is likely to operate as a unilateral act of transfer of a female for marriage to an opposite marriageable group. Although the act of transfer of a woman in marriage to another family may be unilateral among the educated Mers (living locally or settled abroad), its modus operandi would possibly lead to reciprocity by multiple sources of the *nataria* lineages, as if in an open system of marriage-market, without preferential or prescriptive lables attached to it. This is a kind of structural change which seems to be built into the Mer kinship organisation that becomes flexible under the pressures of hard realities of life and circumstances.

Whatever may be the future of bilateral cross-cousin marriage among the Mers, I am highly impressed by the functional excellence of this system of marital alliances as such, and as a system of social relationship of individuals and groups. The institution of bilateral cross-cousin marriage is a super-excellent mechanical device of efficient social living. Like the universal cycle of life and death, it provides a super-symbolic mechanism assuring recruitment of spouses at the micro-level of family and kin group especially from the point of view of survival of the species. In it are combined and interwoven other forms of marriage such as sister exchange, sororate and levirate. It provides a unique combination of diverse groups of people for the purpose of procreation, and therefore, an organic social entity wherein both *rational will* and *natural will* of man has been fully manifested and clearly expressed. It is the highest ever evolved form of cognitive and creative expression of human relationships and of social existence engineered by the human mind.

If by chance, a large part of humanity is distroyed after the impending nuclear war, it will be the mechanism of bilateral or symmetrical cross-cousin marriage, I think, that would rescue man from extinction and shall be most helpful in preserving and perpetuating the human species and in creating a sane society out of the scattered groups of people surviving somewhere on earth.

Futuristic View of the Mer Society and Socio-cultural Change over Time

Before we briefly summarise here the results of socio-cultural changes among the Mers, we should take note of two quotations from the well-known anthropologist, Edmund R. Leach. What is generalised by Leach seems to be applicable to various kinds of changes taking place in the Mer Society.

(i) "Real societies exist in time and space. The demographic, ecological, economic and external political situation does not build up into a fixed environment, but into a constantly changing environment. Every society is a process in time. The changes that result from this process may be usually thought of under two heads. Firstly, there are those which are consistant with a continuity of the existing formal order. Secondly, there are changes which do reflect alteration in the formal structure."[13]

(ii) "My conclusion is that while conceptual models of society are necessarily models of equilibrium systems, real societies can never be in equilibrium. The discrepancy is related to the fact that when structures are expressed in cultural form, the representation is

> imprecise compared with that given by the exact categories which the sociologist, qua scientist would like to employ. I hold that these inconsistancies in the logic of ritual expression are always necessary for the proper functioning of any social system."[14]

Now, we present in the following paragraphs the significant findings and conclusions of this study with the hope that they will be helpful in understanding the types of changes which will take place in Mer Society.

(1) The most important factor that has created decisive impact on the material culture of the Mers in the last two decades is the rapid introduction of new technology. Geographical condition and ecological situation have retained the age-old dual character of Mer region, and therefore the meaningfulness of its division into subregions viz. : the highland and lowland persist. Taking an overview of the situation however, it should be noted that the impact of "technological vectors" on the socio-cultural changes have imposed certain common living standards on the people of the two subregions but have not eliminated basic points of contrast. Thirty years ago, only a few technological innovations were accepted by a handful of rich Mers, but today their number has increased considerably.

(2) Formerly, it was a big news if a family hired microphones, loud-speakers in order to entertain guests and other villagers at marriage or religious congregations. On such occasions, people were treated with film songs and religious *bhajans*. These media of information are not only used for spreading new knowledge but also for reinforcing old values ingrained in folk-songs and stories of the past. The network of public transport and private taxi and truck facilities has spread out far and wide in the region. The use of electricity or diesel oil-pump-sets, motor-cycles, bicycles has become fairly common. The poorer Mer families organise marriage functions at the Maher Students Boarding House in Porbandar and return to the home village in the evening with the marriage party. The simple Arya Samaj form of marriage ritual has made this feasible, and reduced their dependence of the Brahmin priest. The rich families, specially in the highland, marry their children

with fanfare at the farm-house from where most of the guests are provided with transport facilities to return home in a day or two. In olden times, marriage guests would live with the host family for longer period of time. Value of time has been enhanced due to use of new technology, the old time consuming customs are getting worn out.

(3) The technological invasion on the life of the Mers has been considerably accentuated and accepted in the form of innovative changes in agricultural practices. Besides, there has been a notable adaptation of innovations in the form of new socio-economic and cultural institutions. In the first place, this has happened through the introduction of service cooperatives, banks, schools etc. and statutory bodies under the three tier Panchayati Raj organisations. These activities are spearheaded by the introduction of higher educational institutions, firms, factories, marketing centres and service cooporative societies. There is a dramatic spurt in the spread of education in the region with the painstaking efforts of the enlightened Mer leaders. In the wake of Independence, the first generation of Mer leaders have made great sacrifices in creating thirst for learning and literacy among the people. Though much remains to be done in this field, we have new primary schools in almost all the Mer villages. The branches of commercial banks have been spreading in the Mer region and are being accepted as alternatives to money-lenders for saving and borrowing money in the times of need. Secondly, the better of as well as poor Mers have established contacts with the outside world, spread over many towns and cities in Gujarat, and even with more distant places in the country and abroad.

(4) The respect for legal-rational system of the government has been fully established except in the field of customary law for divorce. It is a formal deed written on paper and is called *lakhanu*. Even today it determines the cases of the acts of divorce, widow remarriage and sexual offences within the caste. Besides there is a rise of more than one voluntary social service associations of the caste men tackling, social problems in the sub-regions of the Mer land. There are a few Pan-Indian Mer social associations also. A periodical named *Mardangi* is

published from U.K. (in Gujarati) and serves the Mer society in remaining united and strong.

(5) The degree of vertical solidarity of the various artisan castes and the dominant food-producing Mer caste in villages has considerably weakened generally both in the highland and lowland areas. But greater disruption of social system has gradually begun in the highland due to gradual dispersal of village househelds to farm houses. The role of Brahmin priest and Baret the genealogist in the lives of the Mers is weakening. On the other hand, the horizontal solidarity of the Mer community has been strengthened through sentimental ties finding their expression in matrimonial and economic cooperation with lesser known families living in distant villages or places abroad.

(6) From the general observation and empirical evidence, it may be concluded that the Mer society is on the threshold of a major socio-cultural change and it is likely to become a super-system and an ogranisation of its own kind. The little tradition of the Mers is in short becoming relatively complex. Differentiation in the values, attitude and behaviour has been taking place slowly but surely. It is adversely affecting Mer material culture, organisational form and social system as a whole, because differentiation leads to discontinuities of social relationships at different levels in the society. The kinship organisation based on bilateral cross-cousin marriage and the lineage structure made-up of unilineal male descent groups have however not been affected significantly. The *mechanical model* of the society continues to be respected by the majority of the Mers who have remained economically and educationally below the mark and therefore are tradition bound. It seems that the elements of socio-cultural differentiation among the Mers have not become so strong as to lead to widespread discontinuities in the relationships of the people leading to reorganisation of the social system as such on a different plane.

(7) The variety of socio-cultural changes observable in the Mer society have created a fertile ground for emergence of a differentiated *statistical model* of the Mer Society in near future. The basic structural form existing in the shape of *mechanical-model* is being affected by the on-going processes of change in

social relationships. It is likely to give way to a new *statistical model* of the Mer society within the constraints of the physiography and ecology of the Mer region. The patent situational determinants of ecological institutional, socio-cultural and motivational factors in the Mer society spurred by technological revolution is bound to high-light the profile of the Mer people on the map of India.

REFERENCES

1. Rivers, W.H.R., *Social Organisation*, Ed., W.J. Perry, Kegan Paul, London, 1932, p. 75.
2. *Ibid*, pp. 75-76.
3. *Ibid*, pp. 211-212.
4. *Ibid*, p. 216.
5. *Ibid*, pp. 219-220.
6. Ghurye, G.S., *op. cit.*, p. 278.
7. Strauss, Claude Levi, *op. cit.*, p. 123.
8. *Ibid.*
9. *Ibid.*
10. Fox, Robin, *Kinship and Marriage*, Penguin Books, Victoria, 1969, pp. 175-184.
11. Nutini, Huge G., "Some Consideration on the Nature of Social Structure and Model Building : A Critique of Claude Levi-Strauss and Edmund Leach in *Claude Levi-Strauss : The Anthropologist as a Hero*, Ed., H. Nelson Haya and Tony Haya, M.I.T. Press, 1970, pp. 100-107.
12. Strauss, Claude Levi, *op. cit.*, p. 128.
13. Leach, Edmund, *Political Systems of Highland Burma*, London, 1964, p. 5. In the latest Indian study, *Caste and Kinship in Kangra*, Jonathan P. Parry, Vikas, New Delhi, 1979, supports the view that any outright changes in traditional social systems are difficult to obtain, see p. 152.
14. *Ibid*, p. 4.

APPENDIX I

SOCIAL STATUS OF THE MERS IN THE WIDER REGION

As mentioned in the Report of the Backward Class Commission, Volume I, 1976 (p. 29), the social backwardness of a community may be on account of a number of reasons. It may be due to defective social organisation, unprogressive social system, bigoted adherence to out-dated custom, traditional mode of life including occupation and other kinds of social behaviour. Even if a community is not nomadic like the Gipsy or Vanzara, it is possible that the original social structure in which a community has to live does not allow it to undertake radical changes in their social relationships with other ethnic groups. It is therefore necessary in this context to ascertain the social status of the Mers in the wider region in which they are living along with a number of other castes and communities. In the case of Mers there is a historical background which gives them a special status in the region. We shall therefore throw some light on the social status of the Mers in the context of different kinds of relationships they have been enjoying in their wider region. These points would cover, (i) Erstwhile State of Porbandar and Mer Bhom, (ii) Sanskritic Varnas and Mers, (iii) Non-Sanskritic Varnas and Mers, and (iv) Pan-Indian Mers and Saurashtra Mers

Erstwhile State of Porbandar and Mer Bhom

As indicated in the Mer Book entitled *The Mers of Saurashtra* of 1961, the history of the Mers is linked up with the rulers of erstwhile Porbandar State which has been merged with the Union of India after Independence. The princely rulers of Porbandar State came from the well-known clan of Jethwa Rajput, also called the Ranas of Porbandar. The Jethwas are reported to have come in direct contact with the Mers at Morbi where the latter ruled in the end of the eighth century B.C. The Mer community later accepted the leadership of the Jethwas and provided military and feudal services to the State. There have been many cases of warfare that the Jethwas had to fight with the neighbouring States in which the Mers figured prominently in the army of the rulers of Porbandar. In 1573 the Mers gave complete protection to the Jethwa Prince who was bed-ridden, where the State of Jamnagar attacked his territory. The Mers played a prominent role in gaining the lost territory of the State after a great fight at the village of Bharwada where about 2,450 of them lost their lives. This was rewarded by a gift of about 40 villages dominated by the Mers. Quite a number of these villages were later gifted away by the Mers to the State except 16 villages where the Mers enjoyed the status of *cirasdars*, until recently. This is in brief the unique politico-social status that the Mers enjoyed in the land populated by them in most of the villages both in terms of number and size of land holdings.

Sanskritic Varnas and Mers

As it is well-known, the Hindu Society is hierarchical and divided into four principal varnas viz. : Brahmin, Kshatriya, Vaishya and Shudra. This kind of four-fold division of the Society was said to have been evolved according to the historical needs of the Society based on occupational division of labour. There was however, a considerable amount of flexibility and vertical social mobility of the people from one stratum of the Society to the other. In course of time, this stratified structure is reported to have become rigid, as a result of which each stratum or Varna was divided into a number of sub-divisions and sub-castes with local variation. The position of the Mers in the Hindu Varna system has been clearly established in the past on account of the fact that their ancestors came from a ruling clan. The role that they played in maintaining the power of the Porbandar State in times of warfare as well as the protections they provided to the Brahmins and other subordinate castes falling in the category of Shudra Varna speaks highly of them. This has been discussed in detail in my book on the Mers (1961) specially in Chapter VI on Religion and Social structure.

According to the social custom prevalent among the Rajputs of Gujarat, the institution of genealogists and the bards has been considered almost indispensable for maintaining their family histories of martial people. The history of the Mers belonging to all the 14 lineages has been maintained by a group of genealogists and bards called *bhat* or *vahivancha*. According to their records the Mers of 14 lineages have been originated either from sun, moon or fire lines of mythological fame. Notwithstanding this traditional high status enjoyed by the Mers, quite a number of them have remained backward on account of various reasons.

Non-Sanskritic Varnas and Mers

One of the striking features of the classification of various kinds of people in Saurashtra, particularly in the Mer region is that certain people of ethnic origin are labled as Mahajan, Vasavaya, Maldhari, Khedut, Katio Varna, Mangan Varna, Tertasali etc. These names each represent a special class of people based either on occupational characteristics or variations in cultural attributes. Such a horizontal classification of the people has none of the features common to Brahminical or sanskritic tradition of Hindu Society. This will be amply clear from the brief description of each one of these classes in the following lines along with the position of the Mers in the regional society.

The people falling in the category of Mahajan Varna are generally Bania or Lohana by caste. A Muslim or a Brahmin businessman may also be included in this category. It is likely that if a Mer becomes a businessman and establishes his reputation in trade, he may be included in the class of Mahajan. Secondly, the Vasavaya are the people who belong to a number of service-castes and artisan-castes falling in the category of Sanskritic Shudra Varna. A lot has been said on this subject in my book on the Mers referred to earlier and I am sure it is clear that under no circumstances any Mer would like to be put under this classification eventhough he might acquire the skill of a mason or mechanic. Thirdly, the term Maldhari refers to all categories of herdsmen and cattle breeders in Saurashtra, such as Rabari, Bharwad, etc. The Mers have also been known as cattle breeders but since their main occupation is agriculture, hardly a few of them who may be living in the hamlets or Nes of Barda Hills may allow themselves to be called by this name. Fourthly, the class of Khedut Varna refers to all categories of agricultural land-holders, including perhaps the agricultural labourers also. The Mers are no doubt mainly agriculturists and therefore, they are included in this category of Khedut Varna alongwith many other communities of Saurashtra and Gujarat, such as Kunbi, Sathwara, Patidar, etc. Despite the rugged region of low fertility in which they are living, the Mers are highly skilled and fairly developed farmers in Gujarat.

Fifthly, the term Katio Varna refers to a number of sub-castes and communities irrespective of their occupational specialities. This class of people is by tradition made up of very sturdy and powerful communities who have sustained themselves by hard labour and skills under different geographical and ecological conditions of Saurashtra. Some of the people who fall in this category are *Ahir*, *Khant*, *Kharva*, *Koli*, *Vagher*, *Miana*, *Mers*, etc. Most of these communities have more or less martial traditions and are good at defending themselves at the time of inter-communal brawls or warfare. The sixth class of people called Magan Varna is made up of people who are by tradition religious beggers. They did not have rigid caste or sub-caste among themselves in bygone days. However, in course of time, some of them are identified as special categories of Bava, Sadhu and are known by such other names. It is quite obvious that none of the Mers could be included in this class except perhaps some of them who might have renounced the world and joined the people of this class of professional devotees.

Lastly, there is a class of Tertasali which refers to thirteen castes or sub-castes of Hindu affinity. The term Tertasali means 13 bowls or metal dishes. This class is so named because of the fact that all the 13 communities falling under this category enjoy the freedom of inter-dining with one another. It is important to note that except the freedom of taking food cooked by each other, they have no freedom of inter-course with regard to marriage. This lays a great restriction on each of the communities of this class, which at the same time, help them retain their own identity and independence in the social classification in the region.*

Pan Indian Mers and Saurashtra Mers

There has been a proverb which says that the Mers are deeply attached to their own land. In Gujarati, it is said, "*Mer ane morala sarakha*", i.e. the Mers and peacock are similar in behaviour and habit. Like the peacock they would not like to migrate to distant places for earning their livelihood. This is why it was said that the Mers are like peacock who are instinctly bound to live their life in a restricted geographical areas.

The position today is radically different than that was obtained in the past so far as the habit of the Mers to remain confined to the same land and territorial limits is concerned. The first migration of the Mers had taken place two generations ago from a few highland villages on account of the encouragement offered to them by the late Nanji Kalidas of Porbandar, a well-known industrialist of Uganda in the British times. The recent exodus of the Indians from Uganda due to political reasons and Idi Amin's short-sighted policy resulted into a number of Mers further migrating to U.K. due to British nationality enjoyed by them earlier. Some of the Mers are reported to have migrated to other countries outside India also and they have formed a kind of Pan Indian Mer Social Organisation of their own.

Many of the Mer emigrants are maintaining their links with the Mers of Saurashtra for the purpose of social inter-course such as marriage etc. However, they have changed a great deal from their brothers at home. As reported by one of the educated Government employee and a leader of the Mer community, a tendency is growing among the Pan Indian Mers to identify themselves as having separate entity. Their children have been fairly educated and are living under technologically advanced

* I have discussed in detail the relationships between several communities of Saurashtra under the scheme of non-sanskritic classification of the Society in the second edition of my Ph.D. study which is ready for publication and which includes data on various aspects of material culture of the Mers, not published in the first edition.

socio-economic conditions. They have thus changed to such an extent that some of them think it futile to maintain old community bonds intact. It is reported that the U.K. based Mer community collected huge amount of donations to be used for the purpose to improve economic strength of the Maher Boarding House at Porbandar which functions both as a hostel for students and Community House of the Mer people in India. In recent times, some of the outstation Mers are said to have expressed the opinion that they would like to retain the funds so collected for their own purpose instead. They would, for instance like to build in U.K. a community hall for dancing and get-together of the community. This, of course, suggests a revolutionary change that is taking place in the social organisation of the Mers in U.K.

The building of a hall for dancing purpose may mean that there is a chance of free mixing of both the sexes at the time of community get-together. This kind of mixing together of the two sexes cannot be imagined possible among the Mers in Gujarat. A generation ago in India even the group dances exclusively of women at the time of Holi festival were not allowed to be seen by menfolk. Notwithstanding this kind of conservative outlook regarding the Mer women in the past is concerned, in day-to-day life, they are quite free and work with men of their own families in the farm-land without purdah. The education among the Mer women has been slowly increasing in Gujarat but of course it is quite low and it is difficult to compare their status with the young Mer women residing outside India.

In the end, one of the major assessments of the social change among the Mers in the Saurashtra region will be to provide information available on the flow of educated Mers into highly advanced professional categories. At present there are a number of medical doctors, practising lawyers, managers of firms and factories as well as administrators and politicians. In the city of Porbandar itself it is reported that there are 10 to 12 lawyers, 7 qualified medical practitioners and quite a number of managers of small or big firms or industrial units. Besides, there are a number of civil, electrical or other categories of engineers, teachers, bank employees etc. who have been employed in the

Government or private sector concerns. The City of Junagadh and other taluka towns can also boast of other professionals of considerable skills.

To top the list of the above professionals, it is noteworthy that in politics, Maldeoji Odedara who was formerly the Finance Minister in the State of Gujarat and Member of the Parliament in New Delhi. In the present Cabinet of the State of Gujarat, the name of Vijaydasji Mahant stands out prominently as the only candidate elected unopposed from the Ranavav Constituency in 1981. Mahant Saheb is holding the portfolio of Agriculture and Ports in the Government of Gujarat. There is also an M.L.A. from the Mer community who has been elected presently and is representing the rural masses in the State Legislature in Gandhinagar. Jivabhai Keshwala is presently the President of the Junagadh District Panchayat Samiti. He held this position earlier also. Similarly Mahant Vijaydasji held the same position for a couple of years. There have been quite a few Mer leaders who were Presidents of District and Taluka Panchayats and Farmers Co-operative unions.

APPENDIX II

SOCIAL ETHICS AND RELIGIOUS BEHAVIOUR AMONG THE MERS

NOTHING is more valuable to a Mer than his personal honour and family prestige. They hold in high respect also the prestige of woman, Brahmin, Bard and the safety of the cow. They have shed blood for social or religious cause. This has been discussed in detalil in my Book on the Mers published in 1961 by the M.S University of Baroda and referred to earlier. It wili be useful here to deal with the subject of piety and crime among the Mers at different levels of understanding.

On the outskirts of most of the villages one finds the *palias* or the memorial stones of persons who met with untimely death specially on account of their efforts to protect the prestige and well-being of the people in general. A number of Mer youths laid down their lives in fighting bravely against the invaders from outside. We shall refrain from dealing with the stories of such brave people in detail here because our main focus is merely to give counter instances of pious and religious people among the Mers in relation to the incidence of sporadic killings due to blood feuds.

Manibhai Vora a well-known historian of cultures and archaeologist in Saurashtra has published brief biographies of eight Mer women in his recent Gujarati book entitled *Sanskriti Puja* in 1979. The names of these women are : Puribai, Rudibai, Mali Veja Sajanya, Sumri, Liribai, Rupiben and Ujiben. It will be appropriate to summarise the general characteristics of all these pious Mer women. They come from a period of about 200 years from now in the past. They were known for sharing their own limited food with stay strangers who might have visited their village under starvation. They looked after even cattle so carefully that without feeding them properly they would not take their own meals. In the leisure period they would keep reciting the names of God all the while until they would fall to sleep at night. None of them were reported to be crazy for leading a worldly life of sensual pleasure like other common women in their community, some of whom play significant role in inciting blood feuds. One of them never liked to marry because her main concern was to look after her widowed old mother while the other one would work hard like a man in the fields to sustain the income of her old parents. The third one decided not to return to her husband's house on account of differences with the latter. She pledged that she would neither take divorce nor would she like to remarry. She became the most lovable person in her parent's village and even mothered other's children. The stories of other Mer women less known or unknown have not been different. But the story of Liribai is outstanding because she not only renounced all the worldy cares but also became dedicated to religious worship. She became the devotee of the saint named Kalyandas of the Mer community and after visiting all the principal 4 centres of Hindu pilgrimage in India, she became a member of the ashram of the saint. The story of Rupibai is also similar but Liribai is known for possessing miracular powers of getting rid of the health problems and financial difficulties of her devotees.

A number of Mer men who have renounced their lives and become religious saints and preachers number more than 10 in the last 200 years or so. They are Charan Kalyandasji Maharaj (Visavada), Komaldasji (Khambhodar), Kevaldasji Sabeb (Khistri), Mastaramji Somvar Guru (Bokhira), Rambhai Bhagat (Modhwada), Bhimabhai Vejabhai (Kothri), Merubhai Bhagat (Mahiari), Swami Atmaprakashji (Bakharala), Maldevbhai Ranabhai Keshwara (Porbandar) and Vijaydasji Mahant Saheb (Junagadh). Added to this list of male saints is the name of a Mer woman named Charan Ram Guru Mataji (Degam). Many of these saints and saintly persons have been responsible for providing stability and a kind of balance in the life of the Mer community.

Many criminal minded and haughty Mers have taken refuge under the preachings of the saintly people and tried to give up whatever the criminal tendency they have had to harbour on account of the wrong deeds of their opponents within and outside the community. It will be interesting to note that the genealogists of the Mers called *bhats* who maintain the record of birth and death of people in Mer families have also contributed a great deal in throwing light on the biographies of saintly and brave people among the Mers. In general however every village is reported to have atleast one or two men or women called *bhagat* who devoted their lives to the name of God

In a recent example of murderous attack by an aggrieved young Mer on an elderly person of the community shows how a man can go from one extreme point of hatred to the other extreme point of remorse and renouncement of worldly life. A decade ago the young man was released by the court of law because the elderly person on whom he had fired and grievously injured, declined to say as to who attacked him. He was thus released by the court of law. This kind of generosity on the part of the elderly victim himself led to the release of the young Mer who would have otherwise got 20 years imprisonment in jail. The young man on being released from jail immediately went to the elderly person, whom he had attacked, held his feet and profusely apologized for his thoughtless and dastardly action. He took a vow there and than not to drink or gamble and devote all his life to the name of God.

A number of Mers express regret that the people in their community who are basically generous, noble and large hearted, are quickly exited, and loose control over their mind and resort to the act of murder or physical harm to their opponents. They think that there is something in their blood which makes them behave that way. A person affronted or humiliated by the opposite party does not take time to think twice or rationalize his behaviour before taking a counter action. The legal rational system of justice which is prevalent in India was handed down by the Britishers. It calls for patience, forebearance and ethical values in practical life so that no one directly takes law in hand and punishes the opposite party in absence of an impartial intermediary. So far as the experience of the Mers themselves with regard to crime and punishment is concerned, they seem to have lost faith in the afficacy of legal rational system to receive balanced judgement. This becomes clear from the opinions expressed by two friends of mine with whom I entered into correspondence on the subject. They have clearly stated in their letters in Gujarati. that if a man is murdered in a broad day light in the presence of others and if the guilty party escapes without being punished by the court of law, how can any one put faith in the power of the court in punishing a wrong doer. In the court of law all the witnesses become hostile over night and provide no evidence so as to help the court in fixing the motive or responsibilitiy of crime on a particular person. However they have given some suggestions which are of indirect application and are presented in the points that follow.

The suggestion for reducing the incidence of crime among the Mers by and large are of long duration because there does not seem any short cut to reaching the goal of a lasting peaceful life. (a) The superstitions and irrational behaviour arising out of old sentimental values and attitudes can be checked only through education in the liberal sense of term ; (b) the ethical values derived from religions should be used to bring home a sense of rationality among the people ; (c) the role of legal rational system of reward and punishment should be equated with the ethical rationality derived from religion ; (d) Young women in particular who have to socialise the children sholud be educated not only in religious and ethical system of belief but also in learning numerous methods of adjustment by keeping in close contact with the women of more advanced section of the society. These are the four conceptual frame of references which can be useful in developing culturally oriented programmes for the Mers by organising folk-songs, dramas, dialogues and debating contests in public in order to help the people get re-oriented to a new set of values, attitudes and behavoural patterns.

LIST OF ILLUSTRATIONS

Sketches Illustrating a Rich Tradition of Folk Art and Craft among the Mers.

(They were prepared by the author during 1952-54)

2

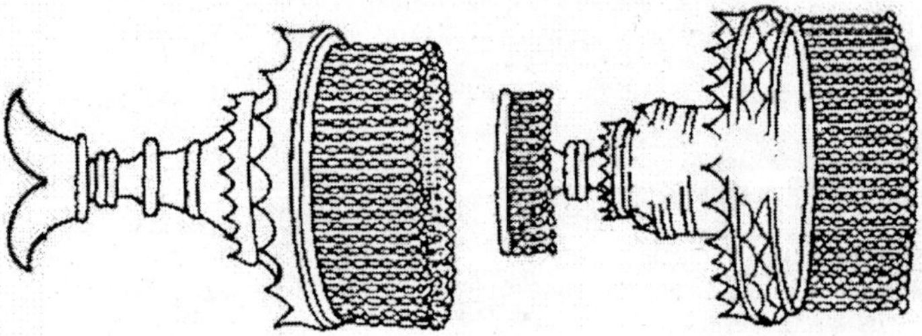

1

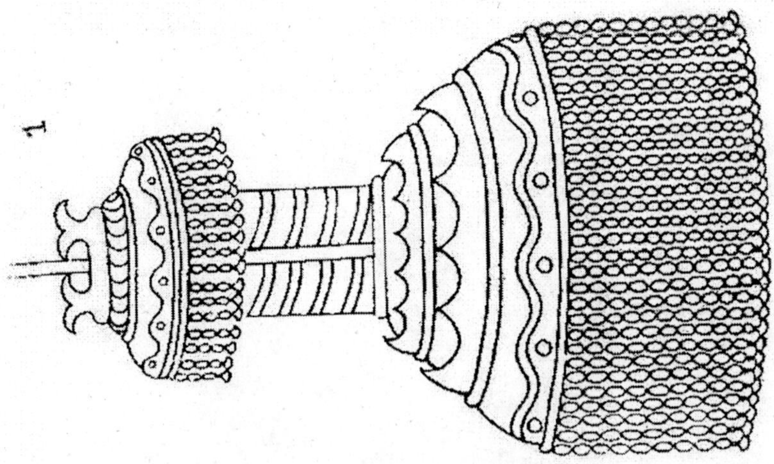

4

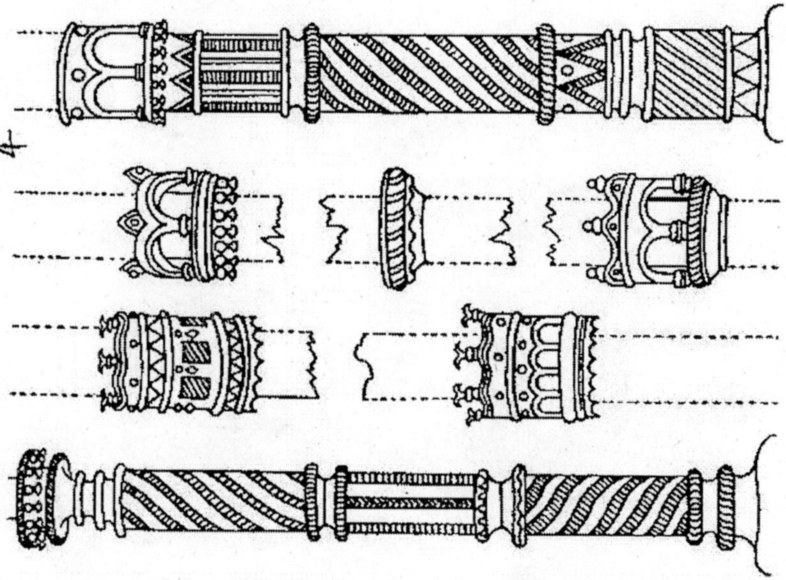

3

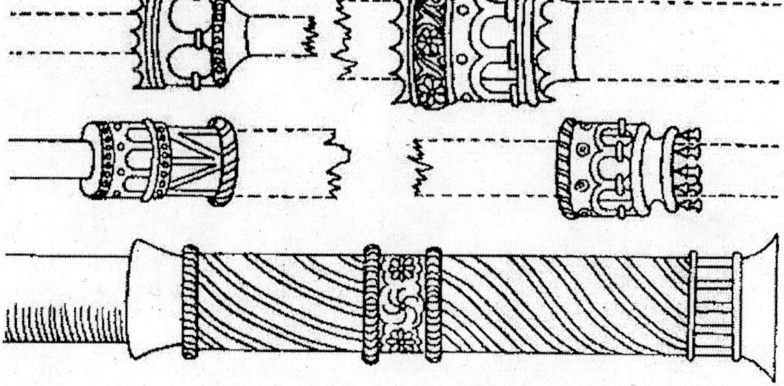

6

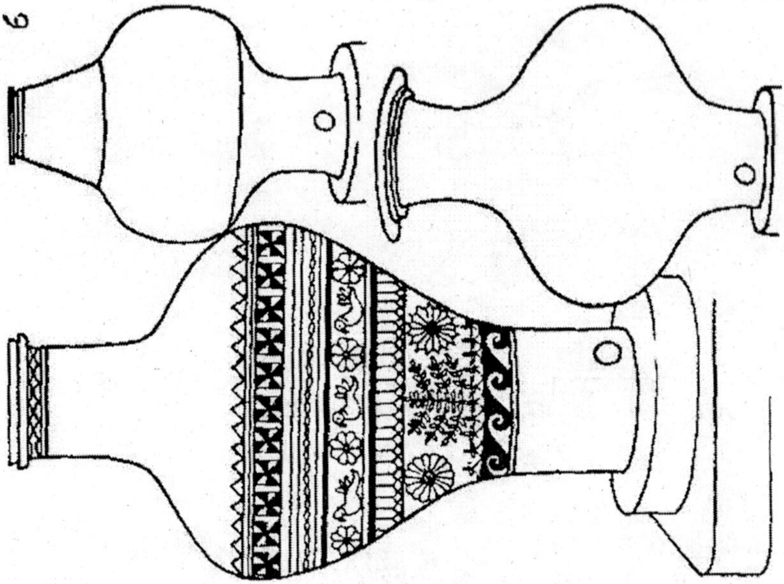

5

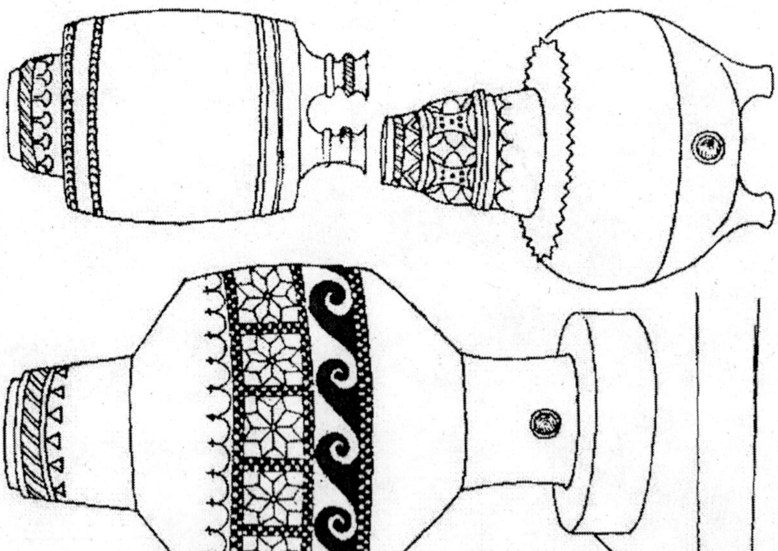

8

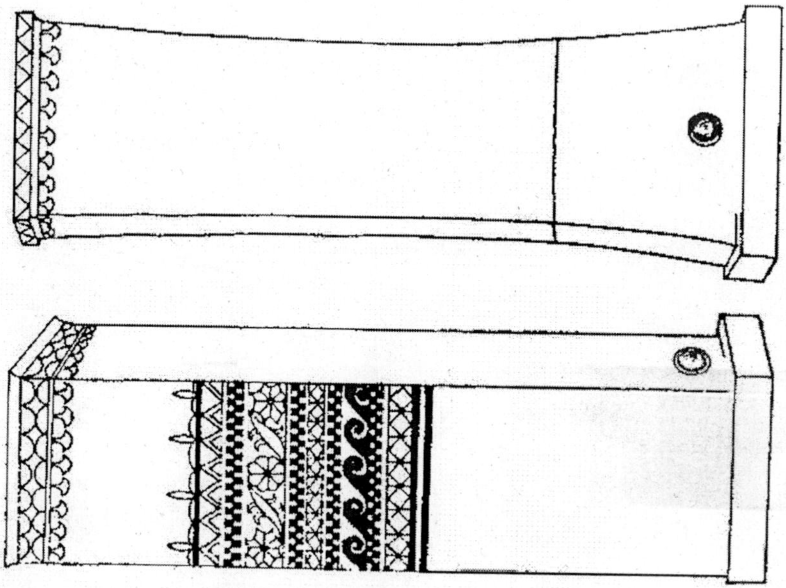

7

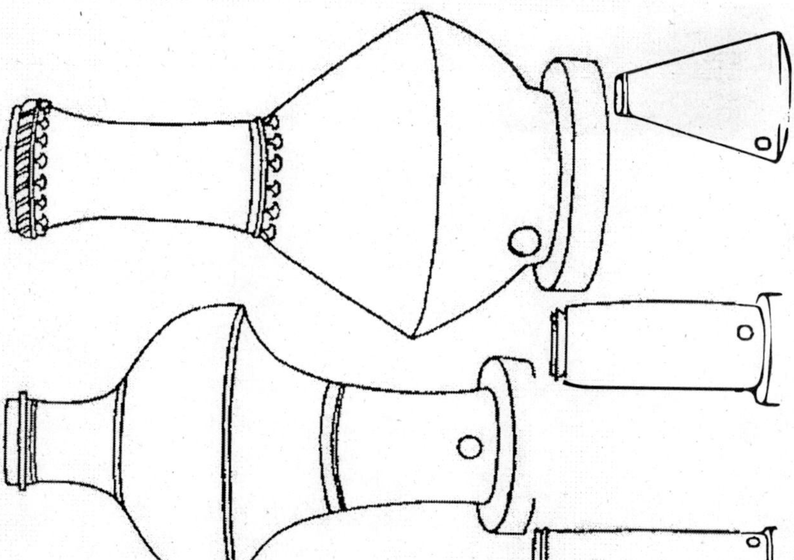

10

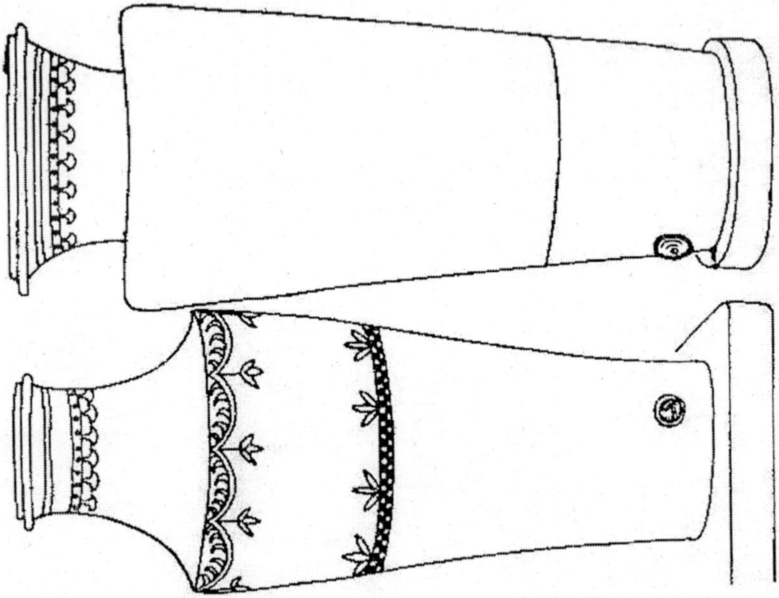

9

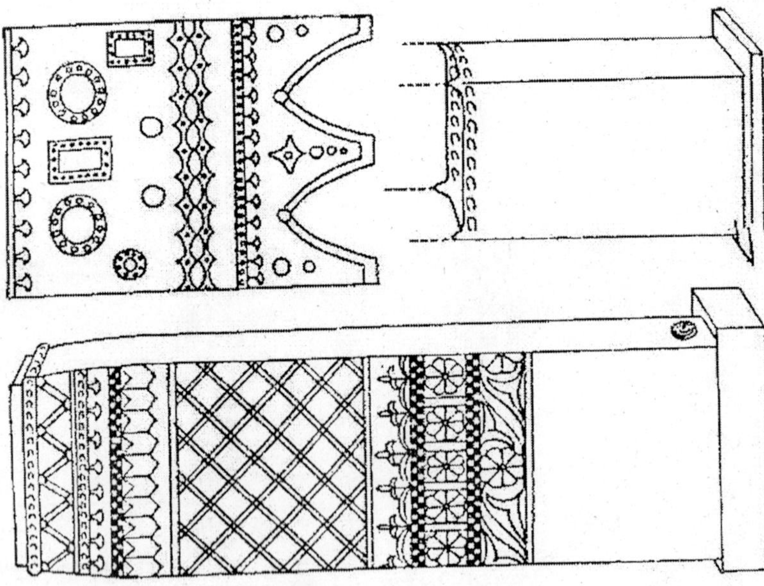

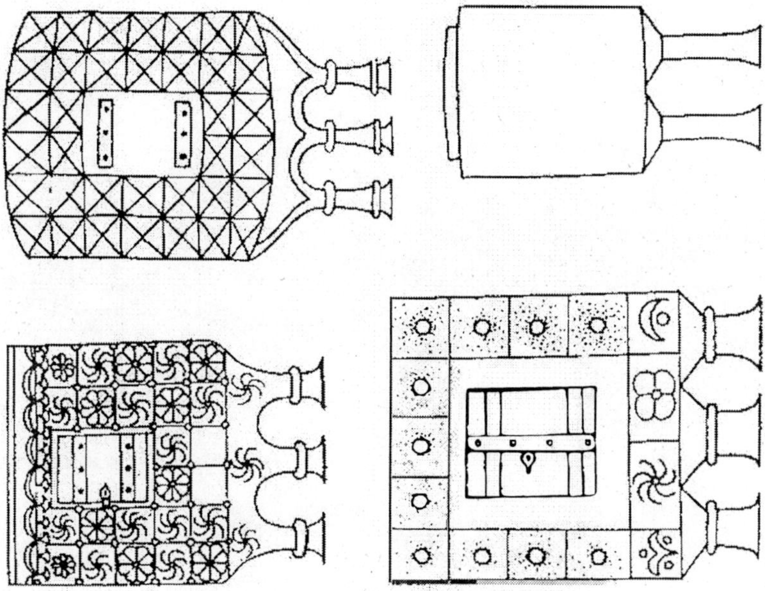

12

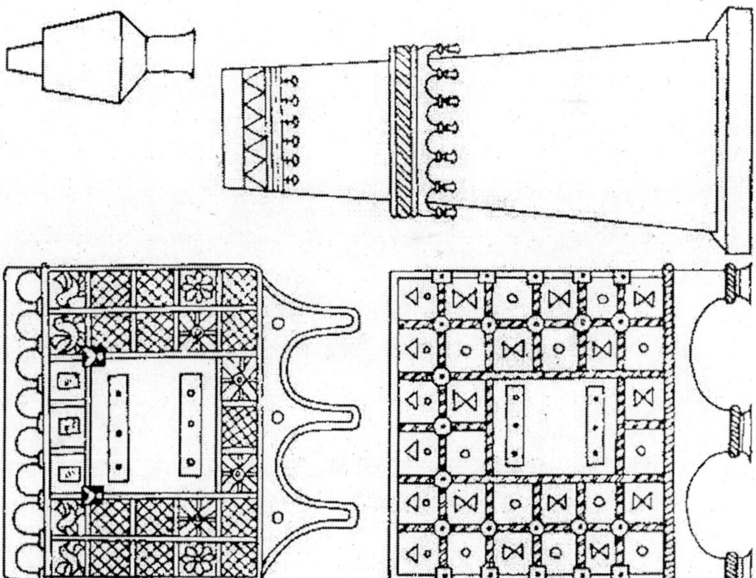

11

14

13

16

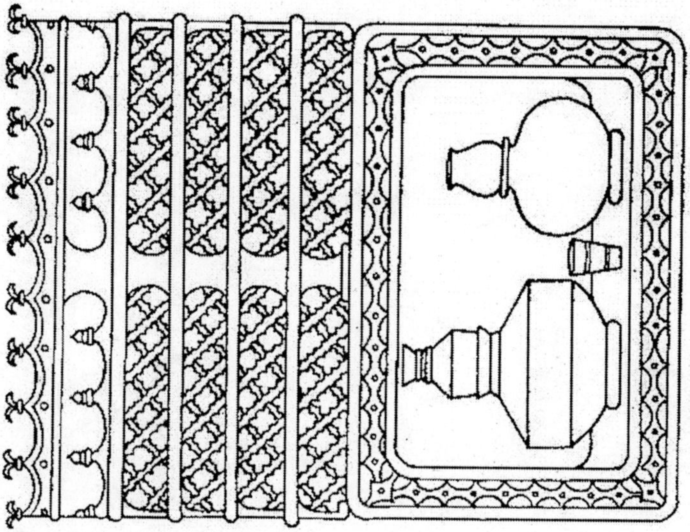

15

18

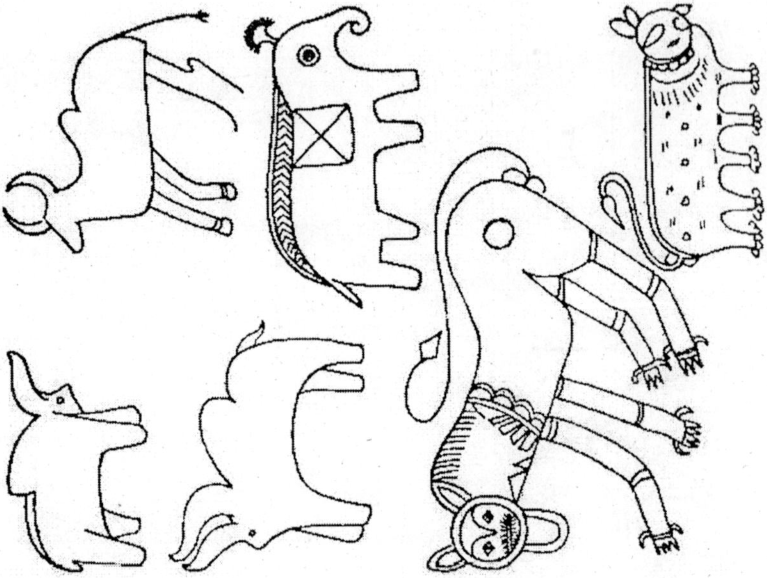

17

20

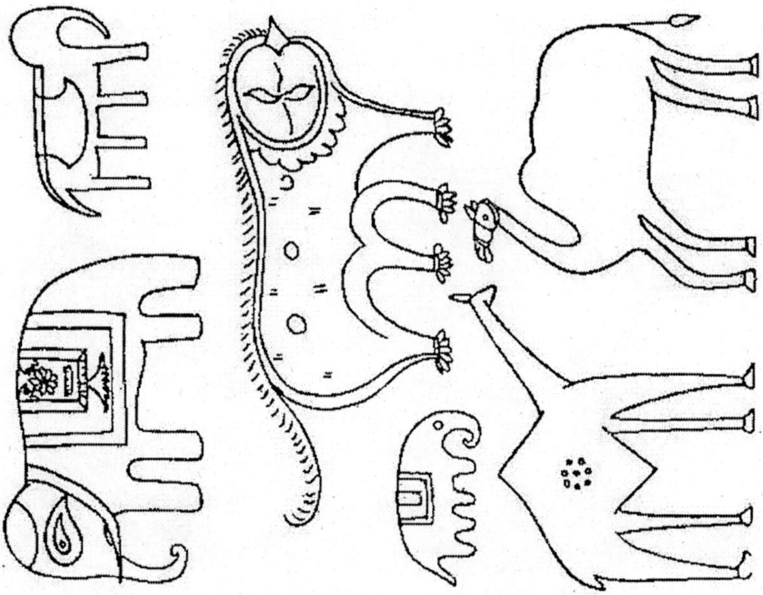

19

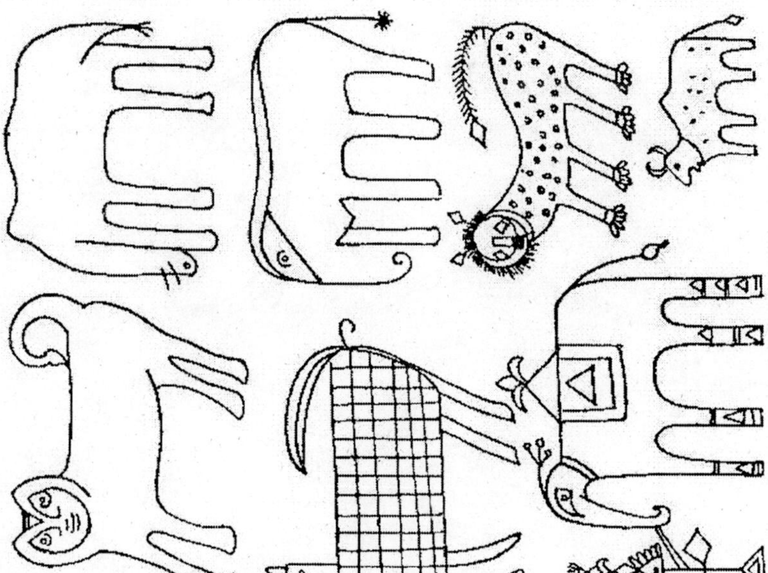

22

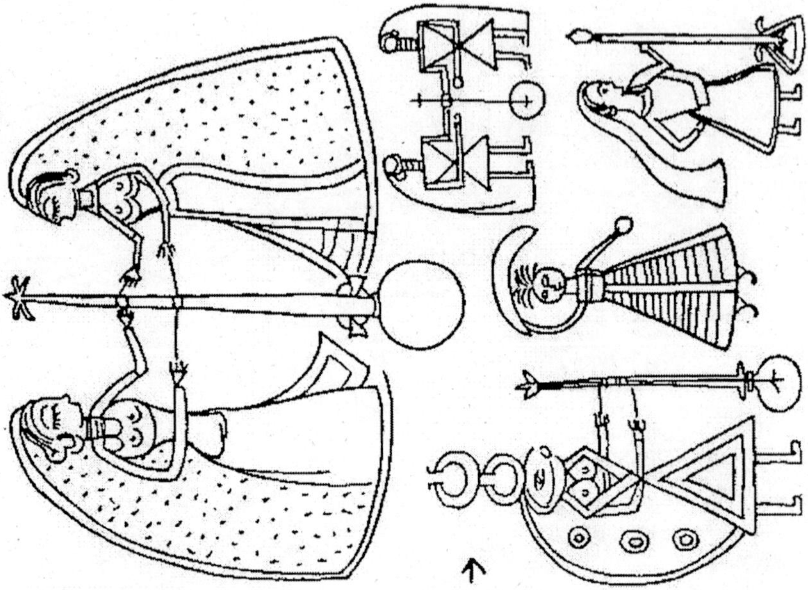

21

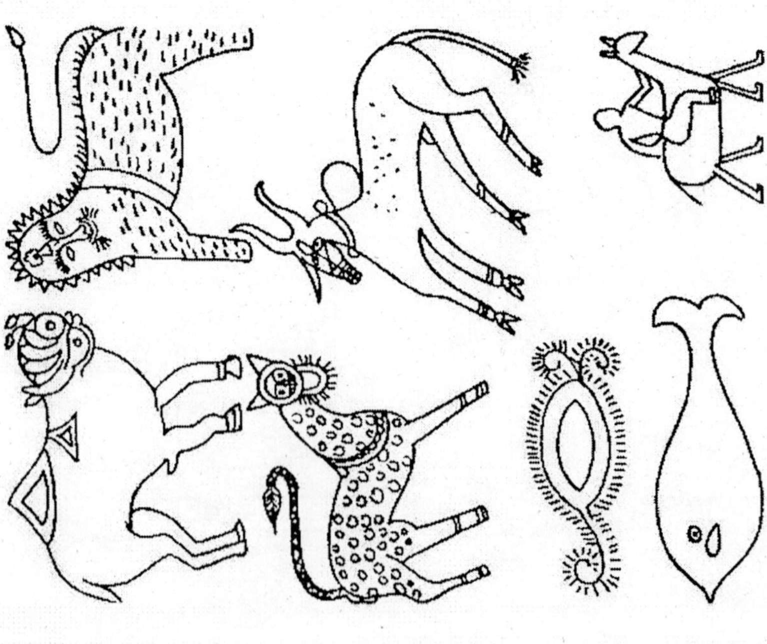

24

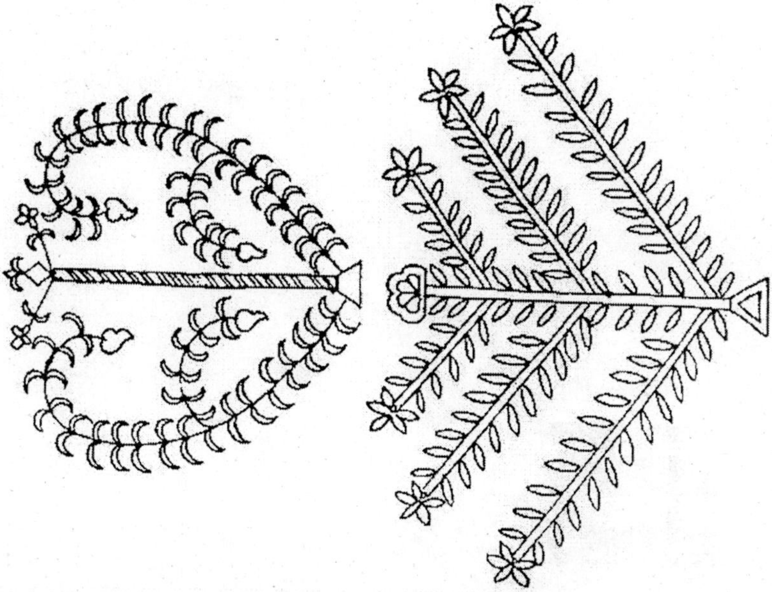

23

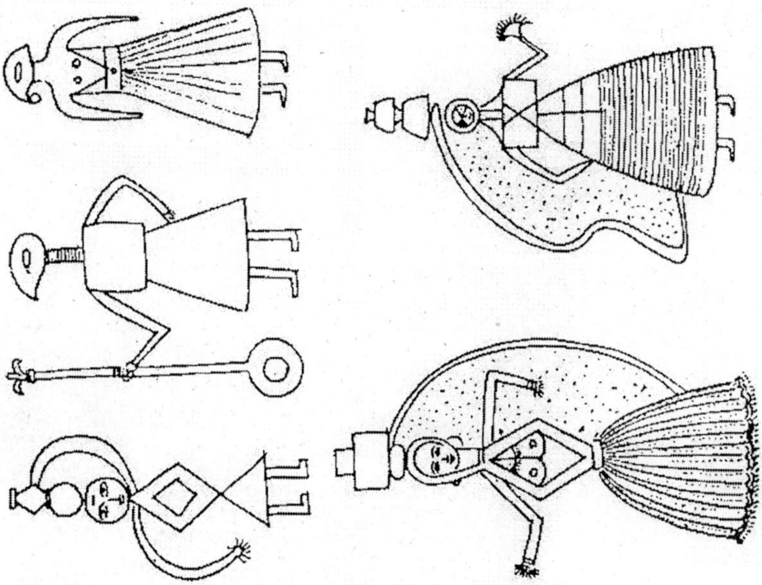

26

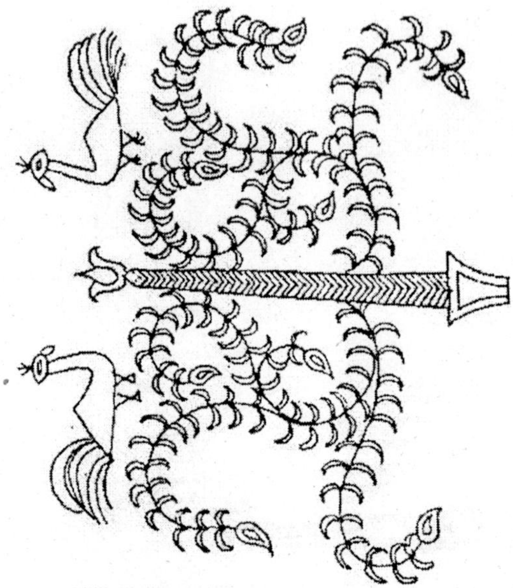

25

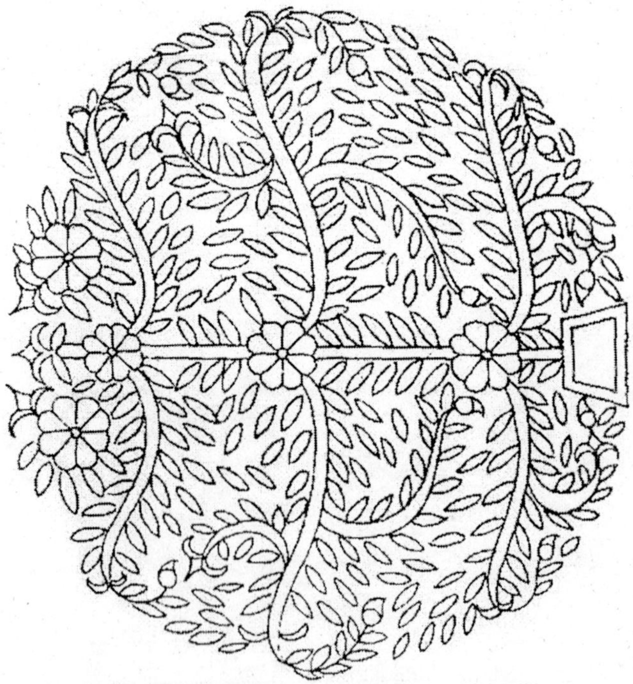

28

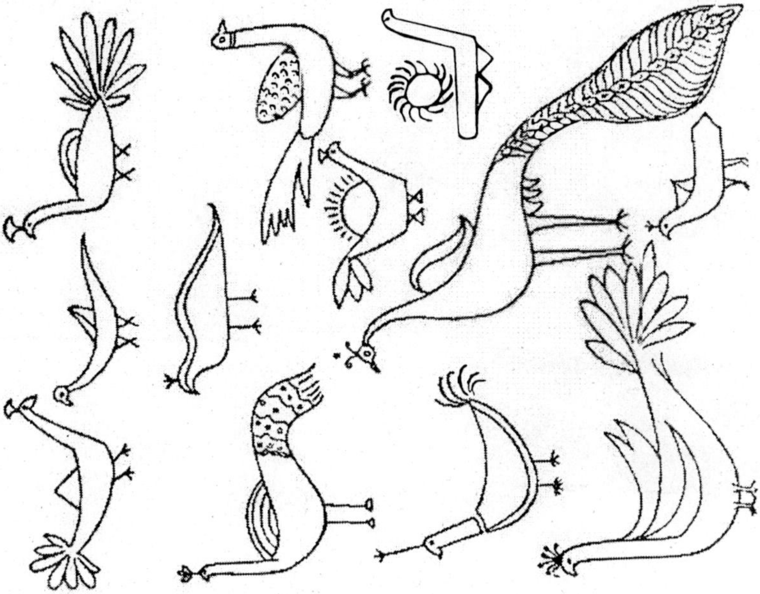

27

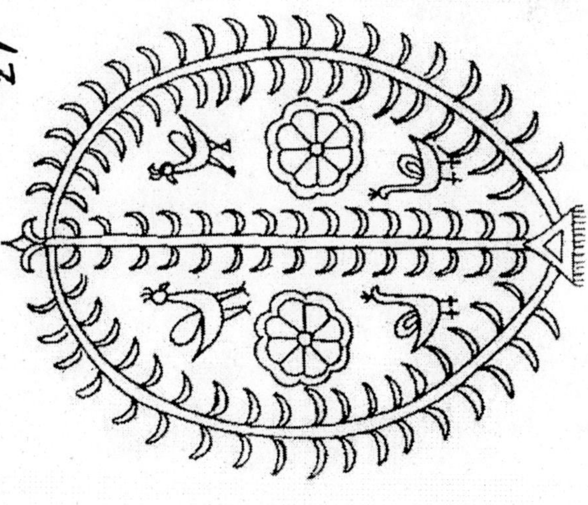

30

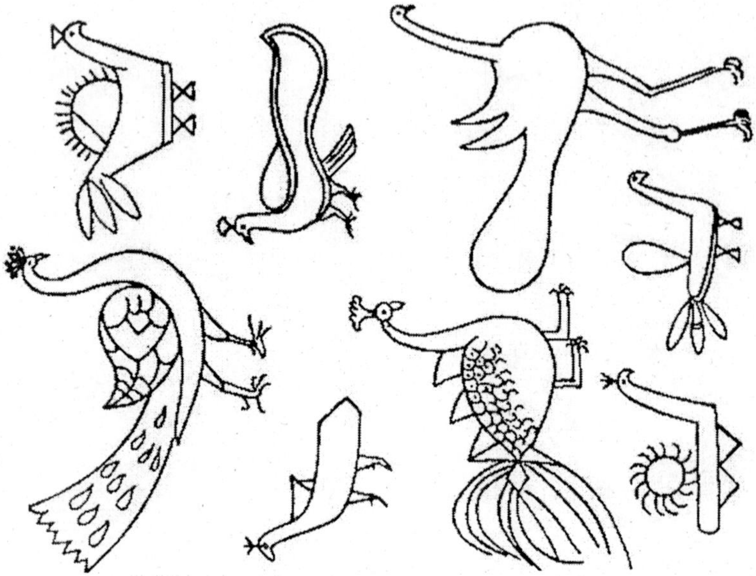

29

32

31

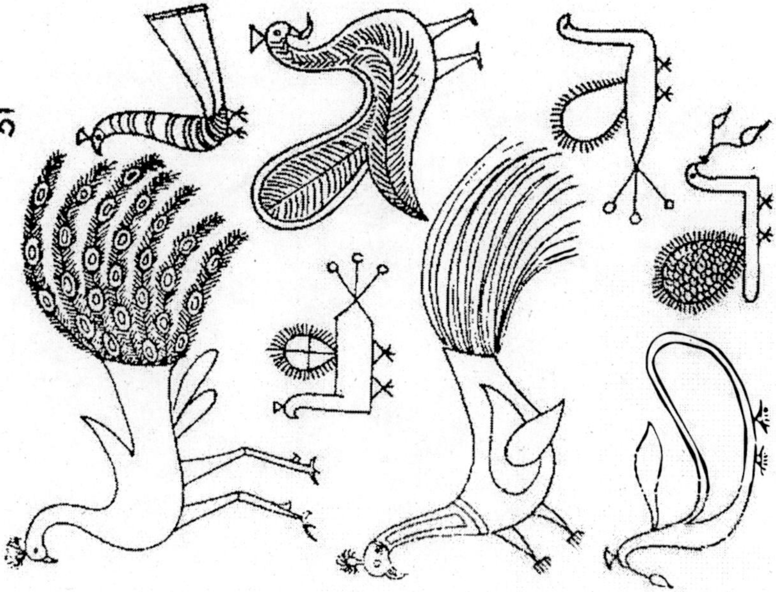

34

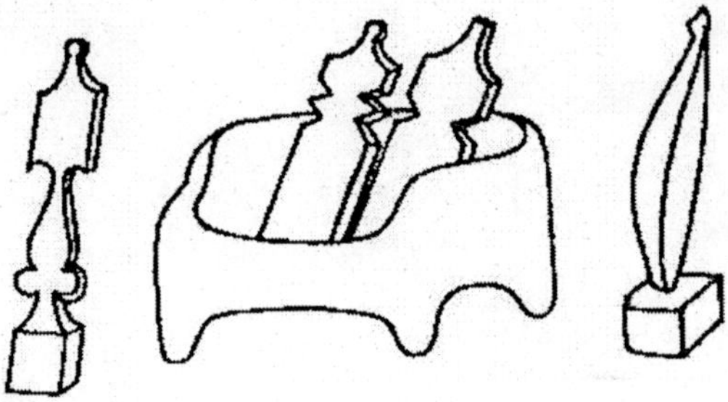

33

36

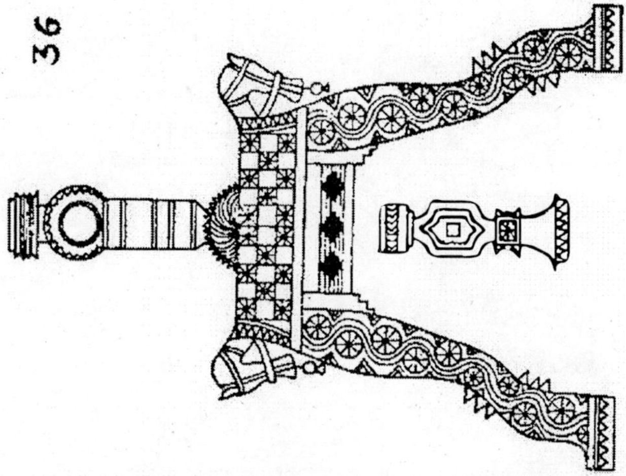

35

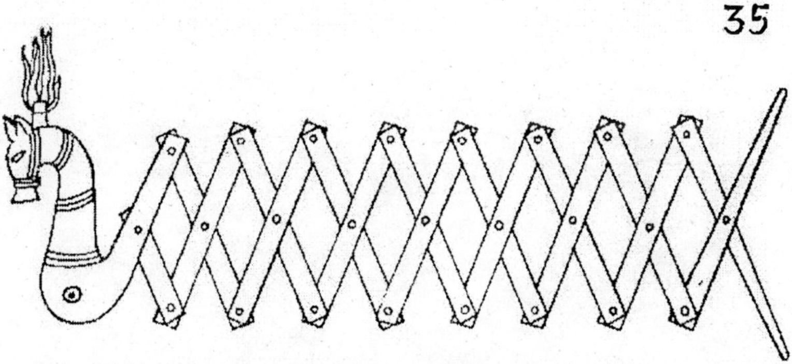

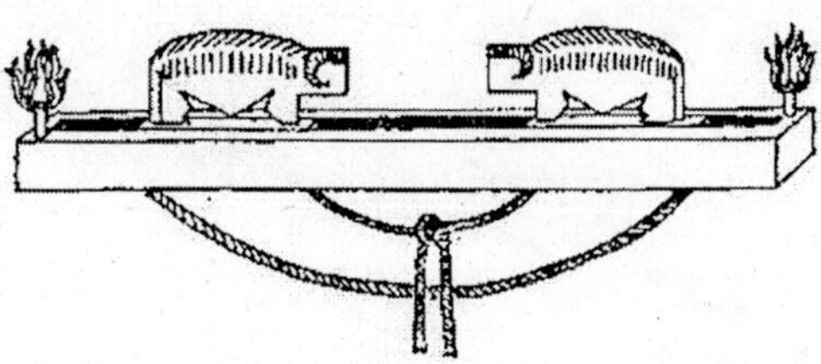

39

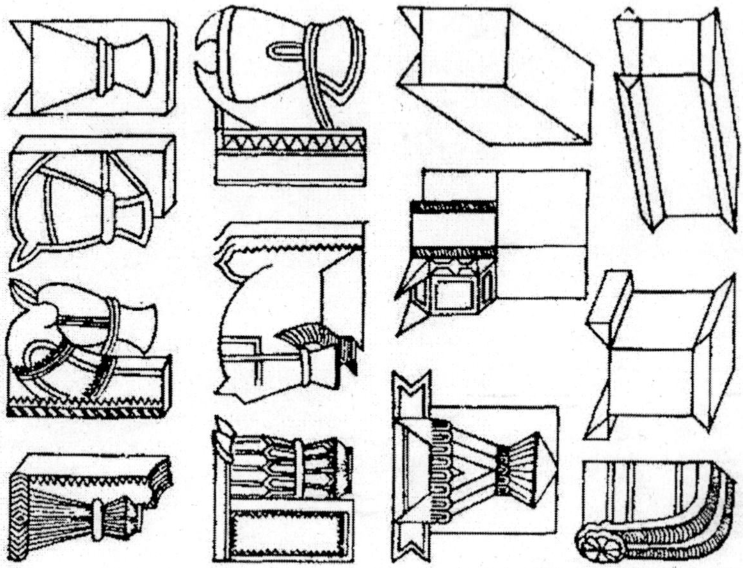

38

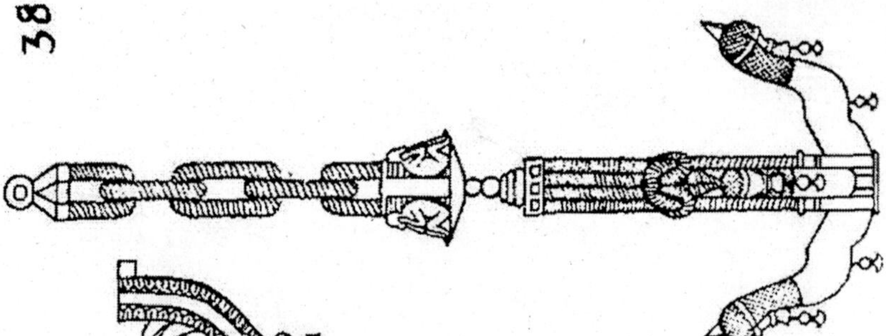

37

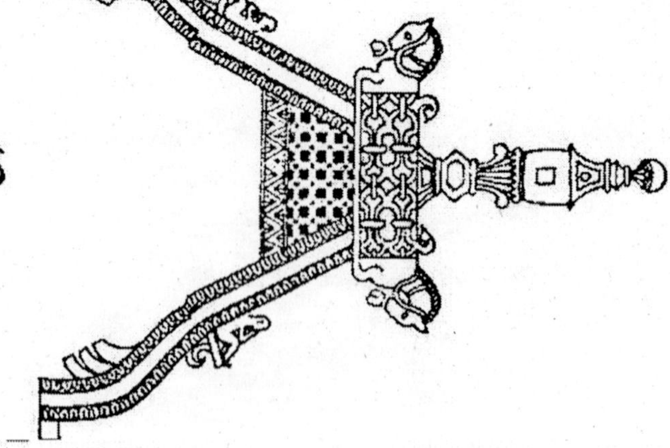

41

40

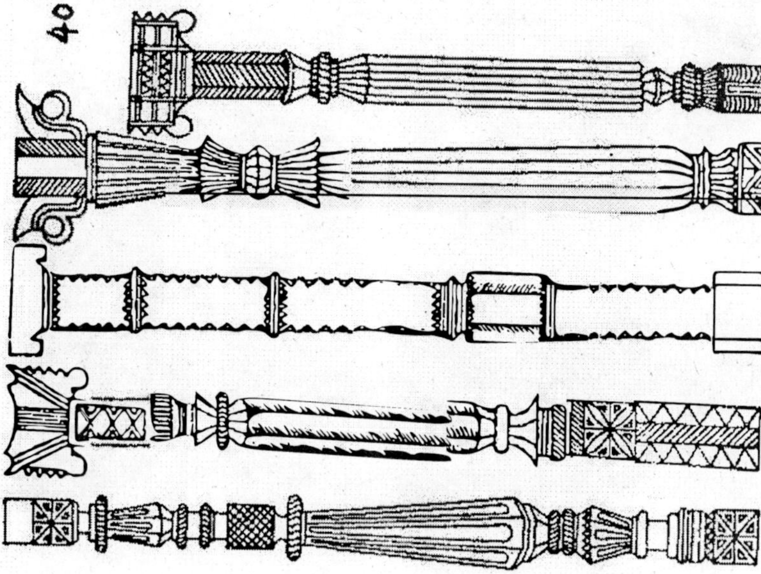

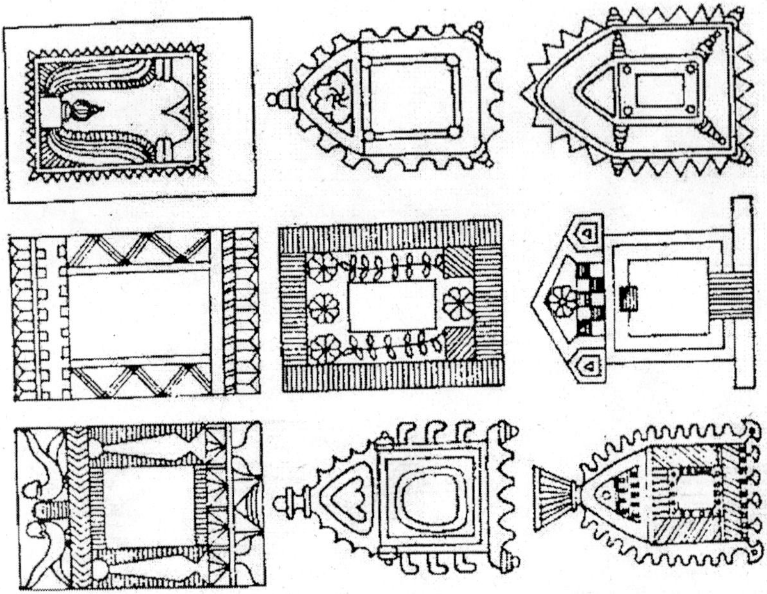

43

42

45

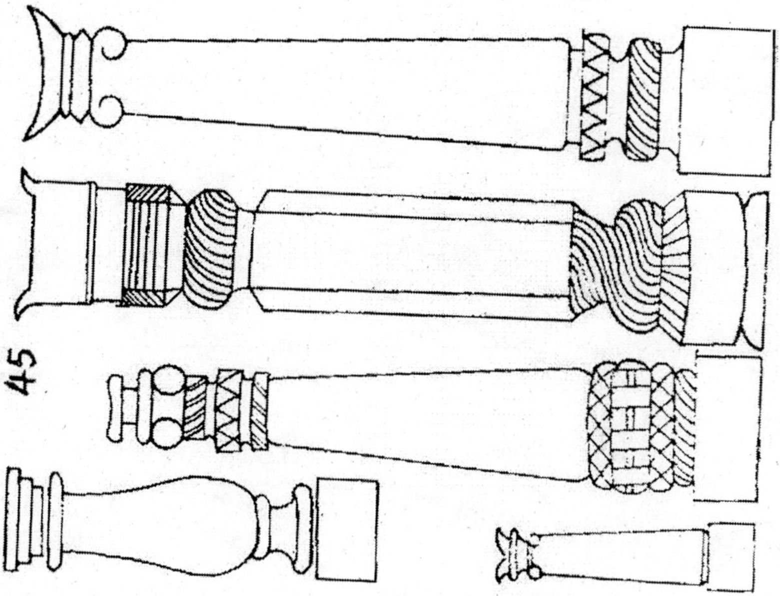

44

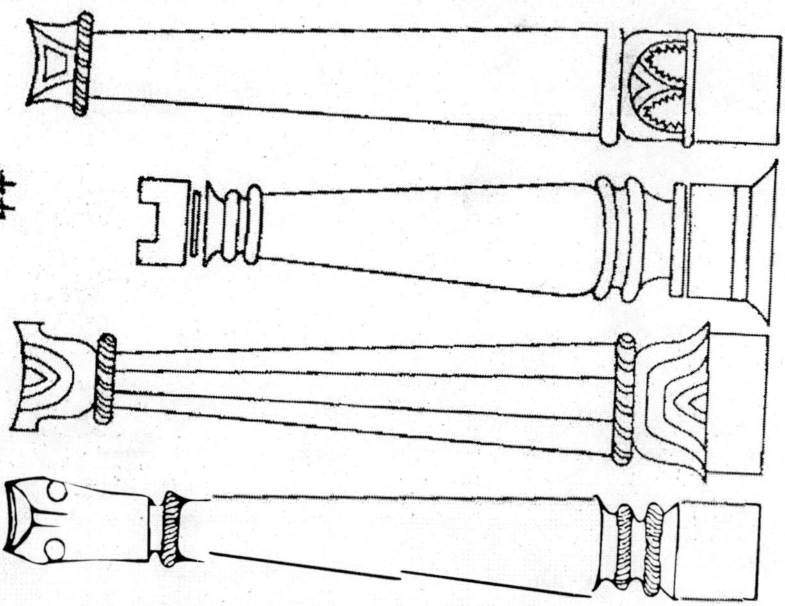

47

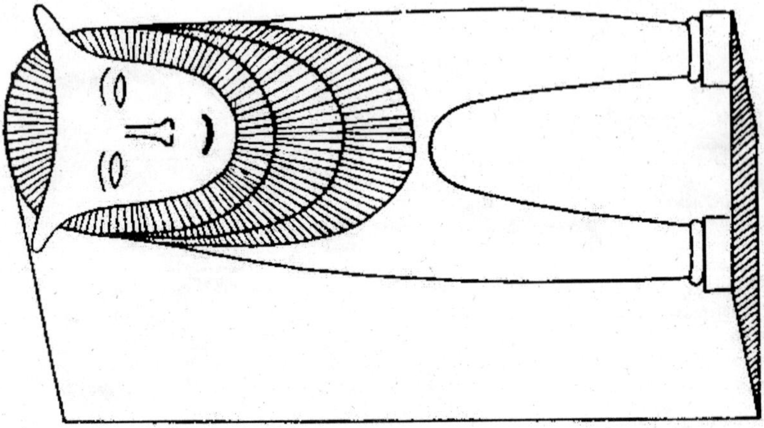

46

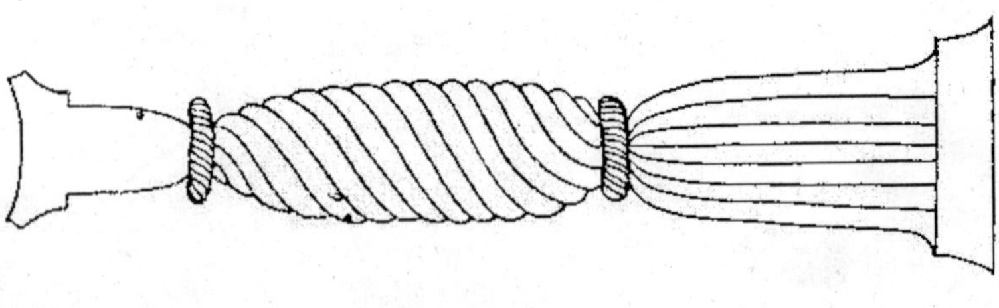

1. Assembly of Mer leaders being addressed by Maldeo Bapu at the Maher Students Boarding House in Porbandar. Vijayadasaji Mahant and Maldevji Odedara are at his left.

2. Author on a visit to inaccessible villages in the lowland.

3. A Mer family with standing crops in the background.

4. A group of women and children on way to propitiate a village deity.

5. A groom with his friends dressed for the matrimonial evant.

6. Marriage ceremony of the bride with the sward representing the groom.

7. Interior decare in the mud walls of a Mer house, in primary colour.

8. Family members taking supper in artistic background of the kitchen.

9. A pair of decorative wooden hangers from a respectable Mer house.

10. A unique death ceremony of earthen pots representing assembly of ancestors.

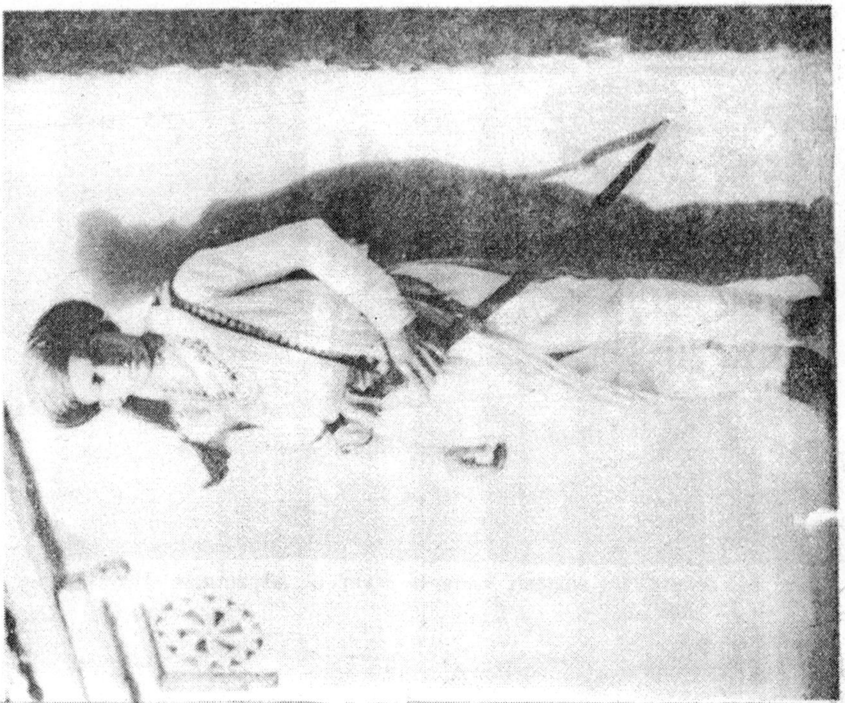

11. A bride-groom in traditional style

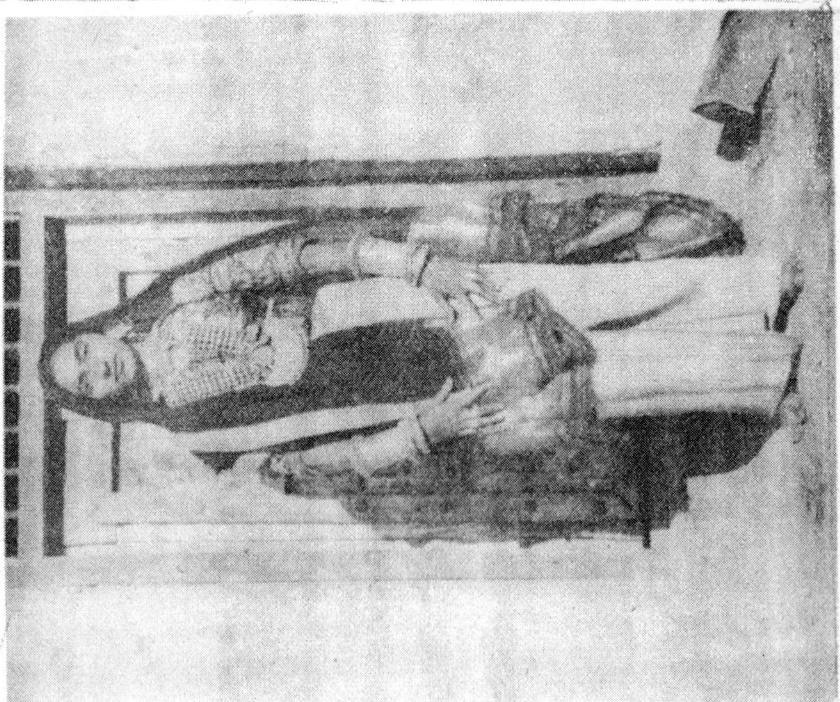

12. A daughter wearing fine dress and ornaments at parent's village

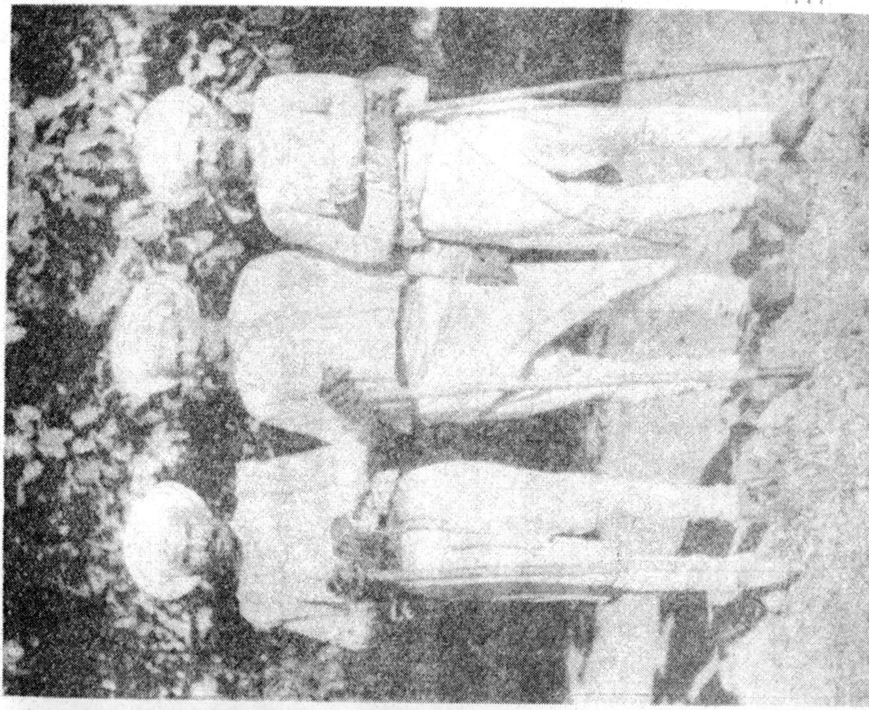

13. Highland Mers

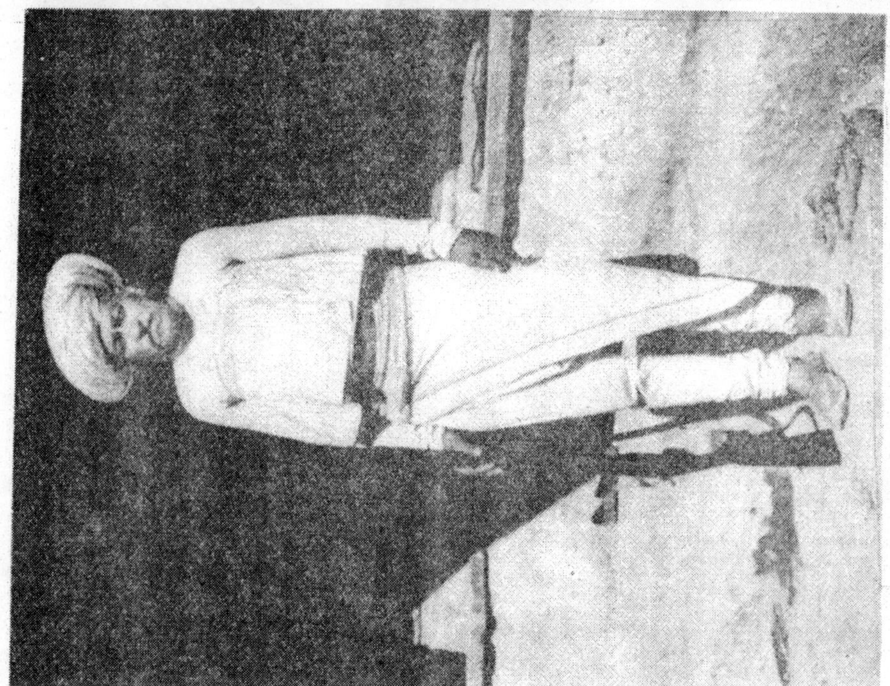

14. Highland older with rifle

15. Old lady wearing fine-wool cover for the Inad.

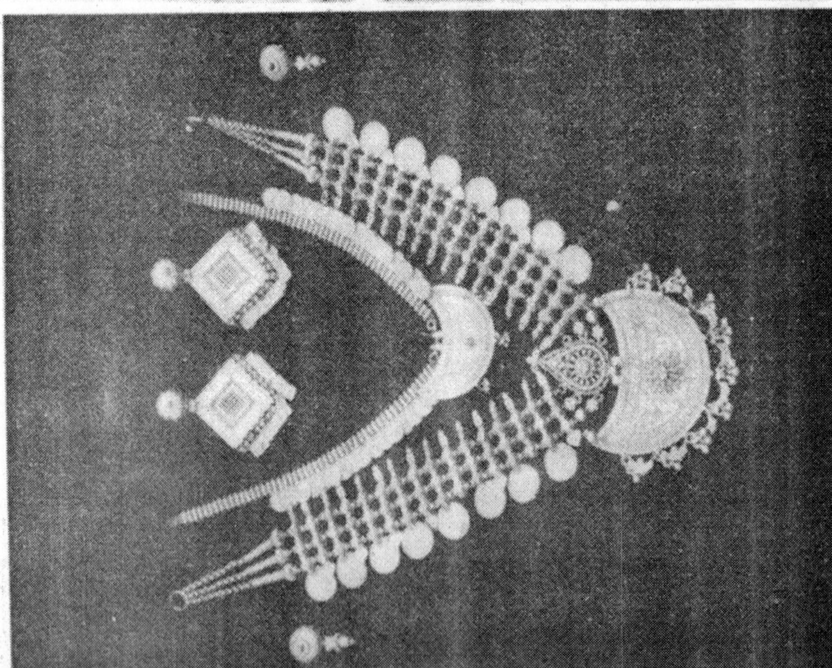

16. Necklaces and ear-rings of gold

BIBLIOGRAPHY

Adya, E. Howard, *Reports on the Economic Geology of Porbandar State*, 1951.

Altekar, A.S., "Six Saindhava Copper-plate Grants from Ghumali", *Epigraphica Indica*, Vol. XXVI, Part IV, 1941, Part V, 1942.

Banerjee, Bhavani, *Kinship and Marriage of Gangadikara Vokkaligas of Mysore*, Deccan College, Poona, 1966, *Census of Porbandar*, 1941.

Dumont, Louis, "Marriage in India : The Present State of the Question", *Contributions to Indian Sociology*, Vol. XI, 1966.

Elliot, H.M., *History of India*, Vol. I, Trubner & Co., London, 1867.

Encyclopaedia Britannica, Vol. II, 1926 and Vol. XIII, 1964.

Fischer, Eberhard and Haku Shah, *Rural Craftsman and their Work*, National Institute of Design, Ahmedabad, 1970.

Fortes, Mayer, "The Structure of Unilineal Descent Groups", *American Anthropologist*, University of Chicago, Vol. 55, No. 1, 1953.

Fox, Robin, *Kinship and Marriage*, Penguin Books, Victoria, 1969.

Fortes, Mayer, *The Wab of Kinship Among the Tallensi*, Oxford University Press, London, 1949.

Gazetteer of Bombay Presidency, Government Central Press, Bombay, Vol. I, 1896, Vol. VIII, 1884. Vol. IX, 1901.

Ghosh, S.C. (Ed.) *The Peninsula of Gujarat in the Early Nineteenth Century*, by James Macmurdo, Sterling, New Delhi, 1977.

Ghurye, G.S., *Family and Kin in Indo-European Culture*, Popular Prakashan, Bombay, 1962.

Gough, Aberle Kathleen, *Dravidian Kinship and Modes of Production*, ICSSR, New Delhi, 1978, Irawati Karve Memorial Lecture.

Gupta, B.A. (with a note by H.A. Rose), "Notes on Female Tattoo Designs in India", *Indian Antiquary*, Vol. XXXI, Bombay Education Society's Press, Bombay, 1902.

Heimendorf, Christopher von Furer, "Comment", *Contributions to Indian Sociology*, Vol. VII, 1964.

Holen, Charles, *Peasant Art in Russia*, The Studio Ltd., London, 1912.

Hoskyn, John, "The Origin and the Early History of the Mers of Merwara", *Indian Antiquary*, Vol. IX, 1922.

Karve, Irawati, *Kinship Organisation in India*, Deccan College, Poona, 1953.

Leach, Edmund (Ed.), *The Structural Study of Myth and Totemism*, Tavistock, London, 1967.

Leach, Edmund, *Political Systems of Highland Burma*, London, 1964.

Levi-Strauss, Claude, *The Elementary Structures of Kinship*, translated from French by James H. Bell, John R.V. Strumer and Rodney Needham, Eyre & Spotiswood, London, 1967, p. xxxv.

Luard, C.E., 'Tattooing in Central India", *Indian Antiquary*, Vol. XXXIII, 1904.

Maldeo, Ranabhai Keshwara, *Maher Javanmarda*, Navaprabhat Printing Press, Ahmedabad, Book II, 1944 ; Book III, 1945.

Michael, J. Mahar, *India : A Critical Bibliography*, University of Arizona Press, Arizona, 1964.

Majumdar, D.N. and K. Kishen, "Aerological Status of Castes and Tribes of Cultural Gujarat", *Journal of the Gujarat Research Society*, Bombay, Vol. X, No. !, 1948.

Majumdar, D.N. and A.R. Sen, "The Anthropometric Status of the Tribes and Castes of Maha Gujarat", The address delivered at the Anthropological Society of

Bombay, *Journal of the Gujarat Research Society*, Bombay, Vol. XI, No. 3, 1949.

Manners, R.A. and D. Kaplan (Eds.), *Theory in Anthropology : A Source Book*, Routledge and Kegal Paul, London, 1968-69.

Mayer, Adrian, *Man*, Vol. 62, No. 164, 1962 (Review of First Mer Edi.).

Mencher, Joan P., *American Anthropologist*, Vol. 64, 1962 (Review of First Mer Edi.)

Mukadam, Debilal, *Mer Jatiki Aitihasik Baten* (in Hindi), Publisher, *Mer Sabha*, Opposite Aryasamaj Building, Ratlam, 1946.

Murdock, George Peter, *Social Structure*, New York, 1949.

Nadavi, A.Z., *Gujarat no Itihas-I* (in Gujarati), B.J. Institute of Learning and Research, Ahmedabad, 1949.

Nutini, Hugo G., "Some considerations on the nature of social structure and Model building : A critique of Claude Levi-Strauss and Edmund Leach", in *Claude Levi-Strauss : The Anthropologist as a Hero*, Ed. H. Belson Haye and Tony Haye, M.I.T., 1970.

Parry, Jonathan P., *Caste and Kinship in Kangra*, Vikas, New Delhi, 1979.

Parsons, Talcott, *The Social System*. The Free Press, Illionois, 1952.

Patel, B.R., *Land Reform Legislation in Saurashtra*, Jamnagar, 1952.

Porbandar State Directory, Vol. I, 1917.

Rao, M.S.A., "Analytical Field Work in Sociologv", *The Economic Weekly*, Bombay, January 20, 1962.

Rao, B. Subba, *Baroda through the Ages*, the M.S. University of Baroda Press, Baroda, 1953.

Richards, F.J., "Geographical Factors in Indian Archaeology", *Indian Antiquary*, Bombay Education Society's Press, Bombay, Vol. LXI, 1933.

Rowe, William L., "Mobility in the Nineteenth century

Caste System", *Structure and Change in Indian Society*, Editors, Milton Singer and Bernard Cohn, Chicago, 1968.

Rivers, W.H.R., *Social Organisation* W.J. Perry, (Ed.) Kegan Paul, London, 1932.

Roth, Walter E., *Ethnographical Studies among the North-West-Central Queensland Aborigins*, Edmund Gregory, Brisben, 1897.

Scala, "German Panorama Barbarossa's Gala Show", No. 7, 1977.

Sohwartzerg, Joseph E., (Ed.), *A Historical Atlas of South Asia*, Chicago University Press, Chicago and London, 1978.

Shah, A.M. and R.G. Shroff, "The Vahivancha Barots of Gujarat : A Caste of Genealogists and Mythographers", *Journal of American Folklore*, Vol. 71, No. 281, 1958.

Shastri, H.G., *Maitrakakalin Gujarat*, B.J. Institute of learning and Research, Ahmedabad, 1955.

Solanki, Asha S., *Gir, Barda ane Alech na Rabario*, unpublished Ph.D. thesis in Gujarati, The Gujarat University, Ahmedabad, 1973.

Srinivas, M.N., *Marriage and Family in Mysore*, Bombay, 1949.

Srinivas, M.N., "A Joint Family Dispute in a Mysore Village", *Journal of the M.S. University of Baroda*, Vol. I, No. I, 1951.

Srinivas, M.N., "Prospects of Sociological Research in Gujarat", *Journal of the Maharaja Sayajirao University of Baroda*, Vol. II, 1953.

Srinivas, M.N., "The Study of Disputes in an Indian Village", *Regional Seminar on Techniques of Social Research*, UNESCO Research Centre, Calcutta, 1958.

Stein, M. Aurel, *Ancient Khotan*, London, 1929.

Sturtevant, William C., "Studies in Ethnoscience", in *Theory in Anthropology*, R.A. Manners and D. Kaplan, (Eds.) Routledge and Kegan Paul, London, 1968-69.

Trivedi, Harshad R., "The Mers of Saurashtra : A Study of their Tattoo Marks", *Journal of the M.S. University of Baroda*, Vol. I, No. 2, 1952.

Trivedi, Harshad R., "Some Aspects of Kinship Terminology among the Mers of Saurashtra", *Journal of M.S. University of Baroda*, Vol. III, No. 1, 1954.

Trivedi, Harshad R., *Mers of Saurashtra : An Exposition of their Social Structure and Organisation*, M.S. University Press, Baroda, 1961.

Trivedi, Harshad R., "Mer Prajanan Lagna Geet" (in Gujarati), *Swadhyaya*, Journal of the Oriental Institute, M.S. University of Baroda, Baroda, Vol. 1, No. 2, 1964.

Trivedi, Harshad R., *A Study of Social and Educational Status of the Mers*, unpublished report submitted to Gujarat Backward Class Board, Gandhinagar, through Institute of Cultural and Urban Anthropology, Ahmedabad, 1982.

Vaidya, C.V., *History of Mediaeval Hindu India*, Aryabhushan Press, Poona, Vol. II, 1926.

Vora, Manibhai, *Sanskriti Puja*, Kadia Plots, Porbandar, 1979.

INDEX